MAINE

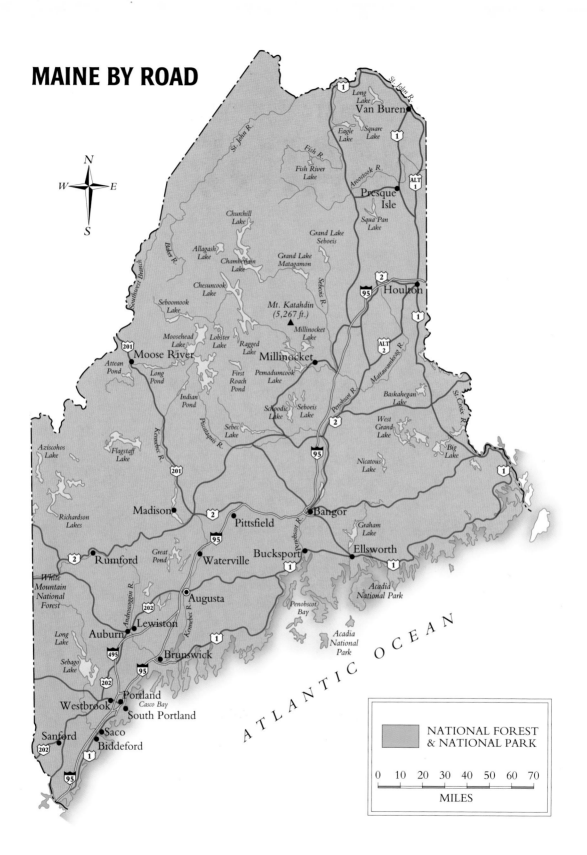

MAINE BY ROAD

Van Buren

Long Lake

St. John R.

St. John R.

Eagle Lake

Square Lake

Fish R.

Fish River Lake

Aroostook R.

Presque Isle

ALT 1

Churchill Lake

Squa Pan Lake

Allagash Lake

Chamberlain Lake

Grand Lake Seboeis

Grand Lake Matagamon

Baker R.

Chesuncook Lake

Seboeis R.

2

Houlton

Southwest Branch

Seboomook Lake

95

Mt. Katahdin (5,267 ft.)

Millinocket Lake

ALT 2

Moosehead Lake

Lobster Lake

Ragged Lake

Millinocket

Moose River

201

Attean Pond

Long Pond

Indian Pond

First Roach Pond

Pemadumcook Lake

Penobscot R.

Mattawamkeag R.

St. Croix R.

Baskahegan Lake

Kennebec R.

Piscataquis R.

Schoodic Lake

Seboeis Lake

2

West Grand Lake

Sebec Lake

95

Aziscohos Lake

Flagstaff Lake

Richardson Lakes

201

Madison

2

Pittsfield

Nicatous Lake

Bangor

Big Lake

1

Graham Lake

Rumford

2

95

Great Pond

Waterville

Bucksport

1

Ellsworth

1

White Mountain National Forest

Androscoggin R.

202

Augusta

Acadia National Park

Long Lake

Auburn

Lewiston

Kennebec R.

Penobscot Bay

Sebago Lake

495

202

Brunswick

1

Acadia National Park

ATLANTIC OCEAN

95

Portland

Casco Bay

Westbrook

South Portland

Sanford

202

Saco

Biddeford

1

95

N
W E
S

| | NATIONAL FOREST & NATIONAL PARK |

0 10 20 30 40 50 60 70

MILES

CELEBRATE THE STATES
MAINE

Margaret Dornfeld

BENCHMARK BOOKS

MARSHALL CAVENDISH
NEW YORK

Benchmark Books
Marshall Cavendish Corporation
99 White Plains Road
Tarrytown, New York 10591-9001

Library of Congress Cataloging-in-Publication Data

Dornfeld, Margaret.
Maine / Margaret Dornfeld.
p.   cm. – (Celebrate the states)
Includes bibliographical references (p.   ) and index.
ISBN 0-7614-1071-6
1. Maine—Juvenile literature. [1. Maine.] I. Title. II. Series.
2. F19.3.D67   2001   974.1—dc21   00-042917

Maps and graphics supplied by Oxford Cartographers, Oxford, England

Photo Research by Candlepants Incorporated

Cover Photo: The Image Bank/Michael Medford

The photographs in this book are used by permission and through the courtesy of; *Corbis*: Robert Holmes, 6-7; Yogi Inc., 10-11; Michael S. Yamashita, 29, 72, 109; Michael Brennen, 55; Kevin Fleming, 58, 82-83; Jeffery L. Rotman, 65; Judy Griesedieck, 70, 107 ; Bettmann85(top), 85(low), 91,127, 129(top), 130; AFP, 86, 125(top)128(right); 89, 125(right); Duomo, 92;Kurt Stier, 96-97; Peter Finger, 99; Farrell Grehan, 100; Wolfgang Kaehler, 113; Jamie Harron;Papilio, 115(right), Pam Gardener;Frank Lane Picture Agency, 118(lower); Bradley Smith, 126; Leif Skoogfors, 128(lower), Richard Schulman, 131. *Voscar,The Maine Photographer*: 14, 16, 19, 21, 23(lower), 24, 25, 61, 69, 73, 75, 76, 103, 105, 106, 110, 111, 115(left), 118(top), 121, 123, 133. *Dean Abramson*: 17, 56, 60, 80. *Photo Researchers Inc/ Alan&Sandy Carey*: 23(right).*The Image Bank*: Joe Devenney, 27; Mike Brinson, 62, 66-67,back cover; Dominic Rose, 63. *Munson-Williams-Proctor Arts Institute, Museum of Art Utica New York, P.C.21*: 30-31. *Maine State Museum, Augusta Maine*: 33, 36. *Pierpont Morgan Library, Art Resource, NYMA.766*: 35. *Maine Historical Society*: 38, 42, 44, 46, 48. *Maine Audio Visual Services*: 50.*L.L. Bean, Inc. Freeport, Maine/1-800-809-7057/www.llbean.com*: 94. *Archive Photos*: 129(lower).

Printed in Italy

1   3   5   6   4   2

CONTENTS

MAINE IS . . .

Maine is a place where dark forests meet the salty sea.

"It is a country full of evergreen trees, of mossy silver birches and watery maples, the ground dotted with insipid, small, red berries, and strewn with damp and moss-grown rocks, . . . the forest resounding at rare intervals with the note of the chickadee, the blue-jay, and the woodpecker, the scream of the fish-hawk and the eagle, the laugh of the loon, and the whistle of ducks along the solitary streams."   —writer Henry David Thoreau

"I love waking up to the fresh sea air. It's invigorating!"
                                                    —a shop clerk in Portland

It is a place where nature mingles with history . . .

"The land was a passion, magical in its influence upon human life. . . . Life ran back and forth, land into people and people back into land, until both were the same."   —author Lura Beam

. . . and people are hardworking, independent, and proud.

"We don't call upon the government for welfare. We call upon our neighbors. If someone is ill, we share food, take care of their kids, and help out. We're natural survivors."
                                                    —Laura Ridgewell, lobsterman's wife

Maine welcomes visitors . . .

"Two or three miles up the river, one beautiful country."
—a Maine Indian, describing the Penobscot River valley to Thoreau

"What happens to me when I cross the Piscataqua and plunge rapidly into Maine at a cost of seventy-five cents in tolls? I cannot describe it. I do not ordinarily spy a partridge in a pear tree, or three French hens, but I do have the sensation of having received a gift from a true love."   —writer E. B. White

. . . and keeps a strong hold on the people who call it home.

"There was a fascination to it: flies and blackflies and mosquitoes. . . . You never shaved and never washed. Why, it was a hell of a place, but nevertheless, you couldn't help but like it."
                              —Frank Dowling, retired lumberman

"I wouldn't live anyplace else but here."   —an Eastport waitress

From its rough-hewn people to its rugged shore, Maine has a simple yet stubborn character unlike any other state. Long ago, its woods and waterways created a booming center for trade and commerce. Today, they attract admirers from across the land. Maine offers a challenge to some and a refuge to others. Let's explore the land- and seascapes, the pathways and personalities that make up Maine.

1 ONE BEAUTIFUL COUNTRY

Maine forms the eastern half of the region known as New England, far up in the northeastern corner of the United States. Its upper half is surrounded by Canada, with New Brunswick to the northeast and Quebec to the northwest. Its long southeastern edge lies along the Atlantic Ocean. New Hampshire, the only state that borders Maine, lies to the southwest.

Maine's rugged terrain emerged 350 to 400 million years ago, when molten rock bubbling up from deep inside the earth pushed toward the surface to form rows of mountains all over northern New England. About 25,000 years ago, a huge glacier spread down from Canada and smothered the land. The movement of this thick sheet of ice over thousands of years flattened the tops of Maine's highest peaks and gouged out its riverbeds. Sand and clay dragged by the ice formed ridges along its highlands. When the glacier withdrew, between 18,000 and 11,000 years ago, the ocean rose higher than it ever had before. The Maine coast that we see today emerged during this dramatic moment in the land's history. Its rocky bluffs and rugged islands are really mountains whose valleys have been flooded by the sea.

THE ROCKY SHORE

Dazzling and desolate, savage and serene, the seacoast is Maine at its most dramatic. Maine's shoreline is long and winding. Measured

LAND AND WATER

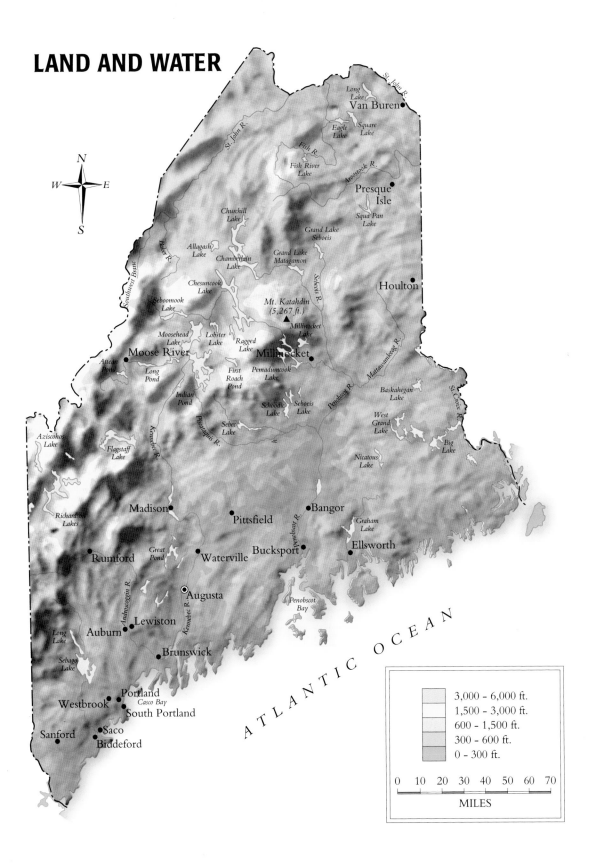

St. John R.

Long Lake

Van Buren

Eagle Lake

Square Lake

Fish R.

Fish River Lake

Aroostook R.

Presque Isle

Squa Pan Lake

Churchill Lake

St. John R.

Allagash Lake

Chamberlain Lake

Grand Lake Seboeis

Grand Lake Matagamon

Houlton

Baker R.

Chesuncook Lake

Seboeis R.

Seboomook Lake

Mt. Katahdin (5,267 ft.)

Millinocket Lake

Moosehead Lake

Lobster Lake

Ragged Lake

Millinocket

Mattawamkeag R.

Southwest Branc

Moose River

Long Pond

First Roach Pond

Pemadumcook Lake

Penobscot R.

Baskahegan Lake

St. Croix R.

Attean Pond

Indian Pond

Schoodic Lake

Seboeis Lake

West Grand Lake

Aziscohos Lake

Flagstaff Lake

Kennebec R.

Piscataquis R.

Sebec Lake

Nicatous Lake

Big Lake

Richardson Lakes

Madison

Pittsfield

Penobscot R.

Bangor

Graham Lake

Ellsworth

Rumford

Great Pond

Waterville

Buckport

Androscoggin R.

Augusta

Kennebec R.

Penobscot Bay

Long Lake

Auburn

Lewiston

Brunswick

ATLANTIC OCEAN

Sebago Lake

Portland

Casco Bay

Westbrook

South Portland

Sanford

Saco

Biddeford

	3,000 – 6,000 ft.
	1,500 – 3,000 ft.
	600 – 1,500 ft.
	300 – 600 ft.
	0 – 300 ft.

0   10   20   30   40   50   60   70

MILES

Waves hit a rocky ledge on Mount Desert Island, the heart of Acadia National Park.

as the crow flies from Canada to the New Hampshire border, it covers a distance of about 250 miles. But if you took out all the twists and turns of its bays, inlets, capes, and peninsulas and pulled it straight, it would stretch all the way to Florida and beyond!

One of the most distinctive features of the Maine coast is the way its stony points and secluded coves crowd together so that the next glimpse of sparkling water never seems far away. Maine resident Harriet Beecher Stowe wrote that as you travel along the shore, "the sea, living, beautiful and life-giving, seems . . . to be everywhere about you—behind, before, around. . . . Now, you catch a peep of it on your right hand, among tufts of oak and maple, and anon it spreads on your left to a majestic sheet of silver, among rocky shores, hung with dark pines, hemlocks, and spruces."

More than five thousand islands dot the Maine seacoast. Some are large enough for hundreds of people to live on, others too small to support a single tree. About two-thirds of the way up the coast looms the most spectacular of these, Mount Desert Island (pronounced "Mount De-SERT"), the main site of Acadia National Park. Waves crash against pink cliffs along the rim of this densely forested cluster of offshore mountains. Its highest point, Cadillac Mountain, towers 1,530 feet above sea level, making it the tallest peak on the eastern seaboard.

The coast to the north of Mount Desert Island is especially wild and lonely. Its rocky shore zigzags all the way out to Quoddy Head, the most easterly point in the United States.

On the southern Maine coast, you meet more people. Maine's largest city, Portland, overlooks breathtaking Casco Bay, about fifty miles north of the New Hampshire border. Farther south, the rocky coast gives way to a mixture of historic seaports, marshland, and sandy beaches.

Long before the first tourists came here, Maine's plentiful fish and lumber attracted ships from around the world. To New England ship captains, Maine was just a quick sail "down east"—meaning east and downwind of Boston. Today, *Down East* is a mood as much as it is a geographical location. It's a term some people use to mean the whole state of Maine and everything that goes along with it. But to most Mainers, the real Down East is the coast—and the farther north and east you go, the more you get that combination of rawness, solitude, and simplicity that gives Maine its distinctive flavor.

NEW ENGLAND UPLANDS

Just inland from the coast and curving north along the New Brunswick border, the land rises up to an area of rolling hills,

Ocean mists cling to Mount Cadillac, Acadia's highest peak.

ridges, and river valleys known as the New England Uplands. Thousands of lakes and ponds adorn this country. Once it was covered by forests, but people have cleared much of the land to make room for crops and livestock.

A checkerboard of woodlands and open fields, the uplands support most of Maine's farms and mill towns. Apple orchards and dairy farms can be found toward the south and around the capital, Augusta. Farther north near the coast stretch the blueberry barrens, where one of Maine's leading crops is grown. But the largest farms sit up at the top of the state in remote Aroostook County. Here the

The blueberry barrens of northern Maine blush crimson each fall.

broad fields between the towns of Presque Isle, Caribou, and Fort Fairfield make up the heart of Maine's potato-growing region. In June and July, potato blossoms blanket the land like a dusting of delicate pink snow.

THE MAINE WOODS

Take any road from the lumber town of Bangor west or north toward the Canadian border and you'll see right away why Maine is called the Pine Tree State. In this part of Maine, known as the Great North Woods, forests cover just about every square inch of land, spreading like a blue-green carpet all the way across the state from the New Hampshire border to Quebec and New Brunswick. In this vast forest, one writer has said, "Trees grow, die, fall, and rot, never having been seen by anyone."

The Longfellow Mountains form the backbone of the Great North Woods. Near the heart of the state rises mile-high Mount Katahdin. Indians once told legends of an evil spirit that guarded Maine's highest peak, but that doesn't keep visitors from climbing it today. "The experience is just too much," says hiker Jeff Wood of Augusta. "As soon as you start past the tree line the hustle and bustle world just seems to slip away. The quiet is overwhelming as the wind passes along the top, it's just you and the mountain." Katahdin's summit marks one end of the Appalachian Trail, a 2,054-mile hiking path that winds through the mountains of the eastern United States all the way down to Springer Mountain in Georgia.

Looking down from Katahdin you can see Maine's largest lakes:

SAVING MOUNT KATAHDIN

Maine owes its largest and most majestic state park to the remarkable generosity of just one man: Percival P. Baxter. Born in 1876 to a wealthy family devoted to politics, Baxter became governor of Maine in 1921. He quickly earned a reputation as a penny-pinching conservative who refused to spend the state's money. But when it came to saving Maine's wild lands, Baxter was anything but tight-fisted. First as a state legislator and then as governor, he kept trying to keep Mount Katahdin beautiful by making it into a state park. Baxter never succeeded, so when he left office he decided to save Katahdin a different way—by buying it himself. In 1930 he purchased 6,000 acres from the Great Northern Paper Company, and he donated it to the state the next year. Little by little over the next thirty years, he bought and passed on to the people of Maine a total of 202,000 acres. That land makes up Baxter State Park today.

When Baxter died in 1969, he knew he was leaving something wonderful behind. He once wrote:

Man is born to Die, His Works are Short-lived
Buildings Crumble, Monuments Decay, Wealth Vanishes
But Katahdin in All Its Glory
Forever Shall Remain the Mountain of the People of Maine

Moosehead, Chesuncook, and Millinocket. Farther southwest lie smaller Flagstaff Lake and the Rangeley Lakes. These stunning bodies of water feed the Kennebec, Penobscot, and Androscoggin Rivers, which tumble southeast and spill into the Atlantic Ocean. Northwest of Katahdin are a series of long, narrow lakes known as the Allagash Wilderness Waterway. These flow into the wild Allagash River and finally the St. John, which marks Maine's northern border before veering off into New Brunswick.

Maine's woods are also threaded with thousands of smaller rivers, streams, and marshes. "I traveled constantly with the impression that I was in a swamp," commented writer Henry David Thoreau, who explored the Maine woods in the nineteenth century. Fed by up to eighty inches of precipitation every year, these forest wetlands make the woods a paradise for all kinds of living things.

PLANTS AND ANIMALS

A rich variety of plants thrive in Maine's cool, damp climate. Of these, none are more striking than the dark evergreens and beautiful hardwoods that make up its forests. Almost 90 percent of Maine is covered with trees. Dark stands of spruce and fir take root in the thin, rocky soil of the mountains, riverbanks, and coastline. These woods merge with cedar and tamarack in low, swampy areas and with hemlock along hillsides. In places where the soil has lots of sand or clay in it, the state tree, the eastern white pine, prevails. Trees that lose their leaves, like beech, birch, and maple, often mingle with the evergreens, and where older forests have been cleared, these leafy trees dominate the land.

"The moose is singularly grotesque and awkward to look at," wrote Henry David Thoreau after a visit to Maine in 1853. Its antlers alone can weigh as much as sixty pounds.

Maine's older evergreen forests are dense, mossy, and encrusted with lichens of all kinds. A typical lichen is usnea, or old-man's beard, which trails in wisps from the boughs of spruce trees. In the spring, fragile wildflowers such as the trout lily, trillium, violet, and pink lady's slipper nestle on the floor of leafy woodlands. Nearby marshes are thick with water-loving plants like bog rosemary, leatherleaf, skunk cabbage, and Labrador tea.

A star attraction of Maine's woods is the state animal, the moose. Standing six to seven feet tall at the shoulder and weighing up to

1,200 pounds, this lumbering giant, with its long, spindly legs and thickset body, seems built for wading in marshes and trudging across deep winter snows. Moose can show up pretty much anywhere in the Pine Tree State, but you're most likely to spot one in the north, along the edge of a lake, marsh, or slow-moving river. They love to snack on water plants and the tender green leaves of saplings.

Besides moose, all kinds of smaller mammals take refuge in Maine's evergreen forests, including red squirrels, chipmunks, and pine martens. Another common north woods animal, the spruce grouse, can be hard to detect, but is so tame that if you come across one, it may even let you stroke its feathers. Also known as a fool hen, the spruce grouse would have been wiped out long ago if it tasted better. It eats so many spruce and fir needles, most animals find it indigestible.

Woodland animals like the white-tailed deer, beaver, snowshoe hare, red fox, bobcat, mink, and porcupine can be found all over the state, from the mountains to the coast. Black bears like to feast on the mountain cranberries and blueberries that grow in clearings. Wildlife thrives on the coast as well. Sea urchins, mussels, starfish, and periwinkles cluster in tide pools—pockets of seawater trapped by the rocks when the tide goes out. Harbor seals cruise in and out of quiet inlets as ospreys and bald eagles soar over the water from the tops of pines.

DOWN EAST WEATHER

"One thing I can't stand is the winters," says a waitress who recently moved from Seattle to Portland, Maine. And it's no wonder—Down

An estimated 25,000 black bears live in Maine. They love to feast on the berries, acorns, and fish found in Maine's woodlands.

A white-tailed deer peers out from a thicket in northern Maine.

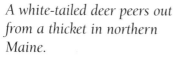

PROJECT PUFFIN

One of Maine's most colorful seabirds is getting a lift these days, thanks to a conservation effort known as Project Puffin. Once a common sight Down East, Atlantic puffins were nearly wiped out in the state in the late nineteenth century, when a craze for puffin feathers—used to decorate ladies' hats—made them a prime target for hunters. The puffins became a protected species in 1905, but they never regained anything close to their former numbers. In 1973 just two fragile puffin colonies remained in Maine, on Matinicus Rock and Machias Seal Island.

Adult puffins usually return to the place where they were raised to mate and start their own families. So a group of biologists with the National Audubon Society got an idea. They took some puffin chicks from breeding grounds in Canada and brought them to Eastern Egg Rock, the site of a former puffin colony. They kept the babies alive by giving them vitamin-fortified fish each day. When the young puffins were ready to leave the nest, they were tagged so they could be recognized later. Between 1973 and 1986, more than 900 puffins were introduced to Eastern Egg Rock this way. Biologists then repeated the project at Seal Island National Wildlife Refuge.

The experiment worked. In 1999, 33 puffin pairs were nesting on Eastern Egg Rock, and 115 pairs were breeding on Seal Island. Maine is the only state in the country where Atlantic puffins breed— as far as Project Puffin is concerned, the more the merrier!

Sledding, skiing, and snowmobiling are popular sports in Maine, where winters can last six months.

East winters are typically long and bitter. January temperatures average twenty degrees Fahrenheit in Portland and as low as eight degrees in the far north. Lakes and rivers freeze over, ice creeps out into the harbors, and deep snows blanket the western mountains. Winter begins in November and can last as long as six months. Most Mainers wait out the last few weeks indoors, marking the days until "ice-out"—that moment when the ice on the rivers cracks, separates, and starts drifting in giant hunks out to sea.

When spring arrives, streams and rivers all over the state swell into a torrent of melted ice and snow. Not so long ago, it was on these surging waterways that Maine's lumbermen risked life and limb driving logs from deep in the woods downstream toward sawmills near Bangor, Machias, and Lewiston. The thaw only lasts a couple of weeks. By the end of May, violet-blue, pink, and white lupines carpet the roadsides along the coast, and the gentle, breezy days of summer have begun.

People flock to Maine from all around to bask in the perfect summers. The only real drawback to this time of year is the bugs: in June and July, the woods are abuzz with gnats, blackflies, and mosquitoes. Out in the open, though, mild, mostly sunny days and cool nights keep the state comfortable all season long. In Portland, daytime temperatures hover around seventy degrees, dropping at night into the fifties. Sometimes a thick fog will roll in and settle over the coast, cloaking the islands in a veil of mystery.

As August turns to September, autumn sets the Maine woods ablaze in magnificent shades of red, gold, and amber. Fall is also peak time for hurricanes, which can slam the coast with winds as high as ninety miles per hour. But when the weather is calm, the cool, crisp days and brilliant foliage can make autumn Maine's loveliest time of year.

Autumn sets the Maine woods aflame with color.

LAND AND PEOPLE

Maine has fewer people per square mile than any other state east of the Mississippi. Nearly half of its population lives along the coast, leaving huge areas in the west and north unsettled.

Yet even in the forests people have left their mark. The 250-foot-tall pines that towered over the land when Europeans first arrived there have long since disappeared—loggers cut them down and sold the wood to shipbuilders back in the nineteenth century. Lumbering, one of the state's biggest industries, still shapes the landscape. In some parts of the forest, Maine loggers use a method known as clear-cutting, where they harvest all the trees in one area at once. This is usually the cheapest way to cut timber, and in the 1970s and 1980s it was used heavily. As a result, many large sections of Maine's woods are stubby and raw.

People have also transformed the state's rivers. About 1,500 dams control Maine's waterways. Although they help fuel the economy by providing hydroelectric power, they can also lower water quality and block the path of migratory fish—fish that are born in the river, swim out to sea, and then return to their birthplace, or spawning grounds, to lay eggs for the next generation. More than ten species of migratory fish once spawned in the Kennebec River, for example, but their numbers have dropped because of dams.

Recently, state and federal authorities made a bold move to help get the Kennebec fish population back up again. Instead of renovating 162-year-old Edwards Dam near Augusta, they simply got rid of it, taking it apart in 1999. Now at least four Kennebec fish species—striped bass, Atlantic salmon, American shad, and

A fly fisherman tests his luck. Efforts to restore and revitalize the Kennebec River are paying off.

short-nosed sturgeon—can reach their spawning grounds seventeen miles upriver from the old dam site. Alewives, which must pass dams upstream, are also beginning to return. Biologists look forward to the day when other species that once spawned at the top of the Kennebec return to the river as well.

2 MAINE, PAST TO PRESENT

Sunset, by Frederic Church

The past is alive in the Pine Tree State. Maine's Native American heritage lives on in the names of its rivers, lakes, and mountains. The state's handsome harbors, quiet coves, and broad inlets whisper of an age when tall-masted ships brought precious cargo from halfway around the world. Even the forests once sheltered hardworking men and women whose stories are waiting to be told.

PEOPLE OF THE DAWN

Historians believe the first people to live in Maine arrived more than 10,000 years ago. Not much is known about these early Maine residents, but it is likely that they used stone tools and hunted caribou, an animal related to the reindeer that once roamed the land in enormous herds. Later on, from about 2500 to 1800 B.C., Maine was home to a group known today as the Red Paint people. They got their name from the graves they left behind, which contain stones and other objects colored with reddish clay.

Many centuries later, the Native Americans who lived in Maine came to be called the Abnaki, which means "people of the dawn." The Abnaki lived in wigwams—cone-shaped houses made of wooden frames covered with bark, skins, or woven reeds. They built their villages along rivers and near the shore and traveled by canoe. In the summer, they stayed by the ocean and feasted on fish,

Maine Indians once tracked caribou herds across the land.

clams, lobsters, and sometimes porpoises and seals. When the weather turned colder, they paddled upriver to hunt moose and trap beaver, otter, and other small game.

Although the Abnaki who lived in different parts of Maine had similar cultures, they came to be known by different names.

The largest tribes were the Penobscot, the Passamaquoddy, the Kinnebec, the Malecite, and the Micmac.

ACADIA

Just six years after Christopher Columbus became the first European known to land in the New World, an Italian explorer named John Cabot, who was in the service of England, arrived in North America. In 1498 he sailed up the Maine coast, planted the English flag in what is now Canada, and claimed the entire area for the English king. Cabot may have been the first European to set eyes on Maine, but no one is really sure. What is certain is that his voyage helped pave the way for the Europeans who would one day settle its shores.

In 1524 another European ship sailed into Maine's waters. Its captain was Italian explorer Giovanni da Verrazano. He was sailing for the French, who also wanted to claim land in the New World. Landing near present-day Portland, Verrazano and his men were amazed by the beauty of Casco Bay.

Many years passed before the next explorers traveled to Maine, though fishermen soon began plundering its rich sea life. Little by little, word spread of the wealth to be found along the coast of Maine and eastern Canada—a region known at the time as Acadia, after a mythical wonderland described by the ancient Greeks.

In 1604 a nobleman named Pierre du Gua, Sieur de Monts, set out from France with mapmaker Samuel de Champlain to scout the Acadian coast. De Monts sailed up the St. Croix River, and his men set up a village on a small island there. While they built houses, planted crops, and got ready to face the frigid Maine winter, de

Italian explorer Giovanni da Verrazano visited Maine in 1524. Finding the Indians there unfriendly, he called it the "Land of the Bad People."

Monts and Champlain traveled down the coast. They came to a mountainous island, which Champlain named Ile des Monts Déserts ("island of bare mountains"), and sailed up the Penobscot River as far as present-day Bangor. By the time they got back to St. Croix Island, de Monts's men were sick with scurvy. Almost half of them died that brutal winter. The rest fled the island as soon as the ice melted, leaving Maine's first European colony in ruins.

THE FRENCH AND INDIAN WARS

The English, too, were determined to gain a foothold in Maine, but it would take another decade or so for their first settlements to take root. Most of these started out as little more than depots where fishing crews stopped to dry their catch before sailing back to Europe. Later, they grew into trading centers for fish, fur, and lumber. Early English settlements like York, Saco, Biddeford, Cape Elizabeth, Falmouth, and Scarborough all lay along the coast, south of the Penobscot River.

Farther north, French fur traders and priests ventured into the woods and became friendly with the Abnaki. By the mid-1600s, the French had good relations with the Indians and controlled all trade along the coast east of the Penobscot River.

With England and France both laying claim to Maine, they were bound to come to blows sooner or later. In 1675 the fighting began. For nearly a century, the French and their Indian allies battled the English for control of the region. Some Maine tribes fled north during the fighting, and some of the French, too, were forced to move. When the conflict finally ended, the English ruled all of Maine.

Europeans fishing near the coast of Maine built fishing stations along the shore so they could dry their catch before the long trip home.

THE NORSE COIN

It's hard to say for certain when Europeans first set foot in Maine, but some people believe it happened long before the 1500s. In fact, some say Maine was discovered more than four hundred years before Christopher Columbus was even born. Scandinavian sagas describe the travels of the Vikings, northern Europeans who sailed the Atlantic Ocean a thousand years ago. According to one story, after Viking explorer Leif Eriksson landed in Greenland around A.D. 1000, he sailed west and started a colony called Vinland the Good. Traces of Vinland have been discovered at a place called L'Anse aux Meadows in Newfoundland, Canada. From there, the Vikings may have traveled south as far as Maine. One reason to think so is a coin that lay buried for centuries under Naskeag Point in Brooklin. Discovered in 1957, this little piece of blackened silver, about the size of a dime, didn't look like much at first. But an expert later confirmed it was minted under the reign of King Olav Kyrre, who ruled Norway from A.D. 1066 to 1093. The Norse coin is the oldest European object ever found in the United States. Did Vikings bring it? We may never know.

REVOLUTION

After the French and Indian Wars, Maine's towns and villages mushroomed. Frontiersmen cleared land and planted farms in the Kennebec and Penobscot River valleys. Maine was now part of the Massachusetts Bay Colony, and in 1770, twenty-seven Maine towns gained the right to send representatives to Boston to help make the colony's laws.

Five years later America launched the War of Independence, and

During the American Revolution, the British nearly demolished the town of Falmouth. Mainers later rebuilt it and changed its name to Portland.

Mainers quickly answered the call to arms. In 1775 near the coastal town of Machias, Maine patriots seized a British ship called the *Margaretta*, beating the British in the first naval battle of the war. Maine suffered badly in the struggle that followed, as British cannons battered its shores. Early in the war its largest town, Falmouth, was bombarded and nearly burned to the ground. By the time the American Revolution ended in September 1783, Maine's ports lay in ruins.

THE STATE OF MAINE

Now part of the United States of America, Maine tried hard to rebuild its shattered sea trade. Falmouth rose from the ashes, and in 1786 it was renamed Portland. As Maine strove to recover, it got little help from the government in Boston, for the war had left Massachusetts deeply in debt. To raise money, the state sold large pieces of property in Maine to wealthy investors. In the 1790s, the Penobscot and Passamaquoddy Indians, who once owned about two-thirds of Maine, signed treaties with Massachusetts giving up all but a small corner of their land and some hunting and fishing rights. The state soon sold the Indians' land at a huge profit— mainly to lumber companies, which were growing larger and wealthier every year.

These businesses suffered when the United States declared another war on Great Britain, known as the War of 1812. Once again the British invaded the Maine coast, blocking trade in all the harbors from Eastport down to Belfast. The officers who were trying to defend the shoreline begged the government in Boston for reinforcements, but help never came.

By the time the British retreated, many Maine citizens were angry with the Massachusetts government for leaving them stranded in a time of need. Some settlers had been arguing for years that Maine should become a state of its own. They had complained that Boston was too far away, that the people there didn't understand Maine's problems, and that the government taxed them unfairly. Now even more people were beginning to think Maine should break free. In 1819 the question was put to a vote. The "separatists" won by a landslide, and with approval from Congress, on March 15, 1820, Maine became the twenty-third state of the Union.

"THE LUMBERMAN'S ALPHABET"

This is one of the many songs that Maine lumbermen sang to pass the time in isolated lumber camps.

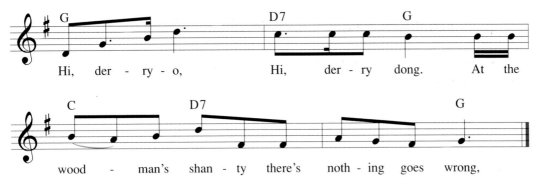

Hi, der - ry - o, Hi, der - ry dong. At the

wood - man's shan - ty there's noth - ing goes wrong,

E is for the Echoes that through the woods ring;
F is for the Foreman, the head of the gang,
G is for the Grindstone that swiftly goes round,
And H is for the Handle so smooth and so round. *Chorus*

I is for Iron, with which we mark pine,
And J is for Jolly Boys, all in a line.
K is for the Keen edge our axes we keep,
And L is for the Lice that over us creep. *Chorus*

M is for the Moss that we chink into our camps,
N is for the Needle which mendeth our pants,
O is for the Owls that hoot in the night,
And P is for the Pines what we always fall right. *Chorus*

Q is for the Quarrels, which we don't have round,
R is for the River, where we drive our logs down;
S is for the Sled, so stout and so strong,
And T is for the Team to draw it along. *Chorus*

U is for Use, which we put our teams to,
And V is for the Valley, which we draw our sleds through,
And W is for Woods that we leave in the spring,
And now I have sung all I'm going to sing.
That's all.

Ships ply the waters of Portland Harbor in the 1860s.

MAINE COMES OF AGE

Soon after it gained independence, Maine's economy boomed. In a few short decades, the Maine coast became one of the nation's most important centers for fishing, shipping, and shipbuilding, and Bangor emerged as the lumber capital of the world. Foreign ships glided in and out of Maine's harbors, and railroads were built, ready to carry passengers from Boston to Portland and beyond. Textile and paper mills sprang up, powered by the state's swift rivers. Immigrants came by the shipload to work in the new factories or in rock quarries cutting granite and limestone. Companies made fortunes harvesting ice from the Kennebec, Penobscot, and Sheepscot Rivers and shipping it in huge cakes, packed with sawdust, to the far corners of the globe. Maine's ports bustled, its towns prospered, and its forests thundered with the sound of falling timber.

In some ways the nineteenth century was a golden age for the Pine Tree State, but the times weren't always peaceful. One problem was that Britain and the United States had never clearly defined Maine's northern border. Both countries claimed the land in the Aroostook territory near Madawaska, an area full of valuable timber. By 1839 the border dispute had become so tense that both sides expected war. Maine prepared to send soldiers to the region and built two military outposts, Fort Fairfield and Fort Kent. But the "Aroostook War" ended before it even began. In 1842 U.S. secretary of state Daniel Webster and British minister Alexander Baring, Lord Ashburton, settled their differences. The Webster-Ashburton Treaty solved the problem without bloodshed and determined Maine's borders for good.

While Maine was defending its claims in the north, thousands of citizens to the south and east were gearing up for another battle. Their opponent wasn't the British this time. They believed they were facing a much more dangerous enemy: alcohol. The world's first anti-drinking organization, the Total Abstinence Society, was founded in Portland in 1815. By the 1830s similar societies had formed all over the state. Their cause, known as the temperance movement, caught on quickly, and in 1851 they persuaded lawmakers to ban the manufacture and sale of liquor in Maine. Though many people objected, this "Maine Law" lasted more than eighty years.

One person who defended the Maine Law was Brunswick resident Harriet Beecher Stowe. Stowe was a passionate supporter of many social causes. Before moving to Maine, she had lived in Cincinnati, Ohio. This was one of the stops on the Underground Railroad, the secret escape route that brought runaway slaves from the South to freedom. Stowe was outraged by the suffering she learned about from escaped slaves, and after moving to Brunswick, she resolved to write a book showing slavery was wrong. In 1851 she published *Uncle Tom's Cabin*, the story of a gentle slave who suffers under the hand of a cruel master. Stowe's novel took the world by storm. Three to four million copies were sold in the United States alone, and it was translated into forty languages.

Uncle Tom's Cabin heated up the debate that was dividing

More than 70,000 Mainers fought for the Union during the Civil War. Pictured here are members of the 31st Regiment, Company D.

the nation. Slave owners in the South insisted their economy depended on slavery; antislavery activists in the North wanted the practice outlawed. In 1861 tensions between the Northern and Southern states reached a crisis, plunging the country into the Civil War. When President Abraham Lincoln called up troops, more than 70,000 Mainers marched south to fight for the Union cause. Maine gave the North thirty-one generals. One of the best known, Joshua Lawrence Chamberlain, a professor at Bowdoin College in Brunswick, commanded Union troops at the Battle of Gettysburg and at Appomattox Courthouse, where the South surrendered in 1865.

VACATIONLAND

After the Civil War, Maine's economy took a downturn. Steel ships reduced the demand for Maine's wooden clippers, electricity threatened the ice industry, and concrete began to replace granite as the country's strongest building material. But very soon, a new industry emerged to take the place of these old ones: tourism.

Between 1870 and 1890, the sleepy village of Bar Harbor turned into a crowded resort where Bostonians, Philadelphians, and New Yorkers gathered for fresh air, sports, and summer relaxation. "A person who had not visited Bar Harbor for fifteen years would have to turn often to the mountains, the sea, and the islands to convince himself that he was really standing on the site of the puny village of that day," observed a Boston traveler in 1891. At Bar Harbor and other seaside communities, wealthy vacationers built lavish summer homes, mansions they called "cottages." Enchanted by the

A century ago, elegant yachts crowded the waters of Bar Harbor, the summer playground of the well-to-do.

beauty of the island-studded coast, they came every summer by steamer and train, whiled away the season yachting, playing tennis, and attending garden parties, then left again when the weather turned cool.

City dwellers eager to get a taste of the Maine woods could

experience them in luxury at hotels like the Mount Kineo House on Moosehead Lake and the Poland Spring House near Portland. Later on, as less well-to-do visitors discovered Maine, rustic cabins, known as camps, became the rage—cozy retreats in the middle of the rough outdoors.

By the early 1900s, Maine had become such a popular vacation spot that some people worried it would soon be spoiled. So working with government officials, conservationists started making some of its most scenic areas into public preserves. The first big piece of land to be protected was Mount Desert Island, the craggy headland that forms the backdrop for Bar Harbor. The island was named a national monument in 1916, and in 1928 it became the heart of Acadia National Park.

INTO THE FUTURE

Maine suffered with the rest of the nation during the Great Depression of the 1930s, when the economy crashed, factories closed, and farm prices tumbled. But its natural attractions flourished under a government work program known as the Civilian Conservation Corps (CCC). The CCC hired more than 20,000 men and women to build trails, roads, bridges, and camping shelters, opening Maine's woods to hikers. In 1937 it was a CCC crew that built the final stretch of the Appalachian Trail.

When America entered World War II, Maine went to work building warships for the U.S. military. Old shipbuilding towns like Kittery and Bath got a new lease on life constructing submarines and iron-clad destroyers. Bath Iron Works grew from a midsized plant with a few hundred workers to an industrial giant employing 12,000. For the rest of the twentieth century, it remained the state's biggest private employer.

Finding the right balance between conservation and growth drove Maine politics all through the 1900s, and it still shapes the state today. Lately, some parts of Maine, like the Portland area in the south, seem close to discovering the key. The northern half of the state has not been so lucky. In fact, these days people sometimes say there are two Maines. The one in the south is modern and

Maine shipyards bustled in the 1940s, as workers built battleships for World War II.

prosperous—the other, in the north, undeveloped and poor. In the coming decades, one of Maine's biggest challenges may be seeing that its bounty is shared by all.

3 MAKING LAWS, MAKING A LIVING

The capitol in Augusta

A favorite Down East catchphrase has it that Maine is "the way life should be." For summer visitors, it's easy to agree. The state's fresh air, slow pace, and enchanting scenery can make it seem like a paradise to people who need to unwind from the stress of Boston or New York. But year-round Mainers don't always have the same ideas about what makes the state livable, or how to keep it that way. They have their own concerns, like improving education and job opportunities and protecting the environment. Maine's government gives citizens a chance to decide what they want for their state and work together to make it happen.

INSIDE GOVERNMENT

Like the federal government, Maine's state government is divided into three branches: executive, legislative, and judicial.

Executive. The executive branch carries out state laws. It is headed by the governor, who makes decisions with the help of a cabinet of experts on major public issues, from education to the economy. Maine's governor is elected by the public every four years. The state's four other executive officers—secretary of state, attorney general, treasurer, and auditor—are elected by the legislature.

Legislative. The legislative branch makes laws and decides how

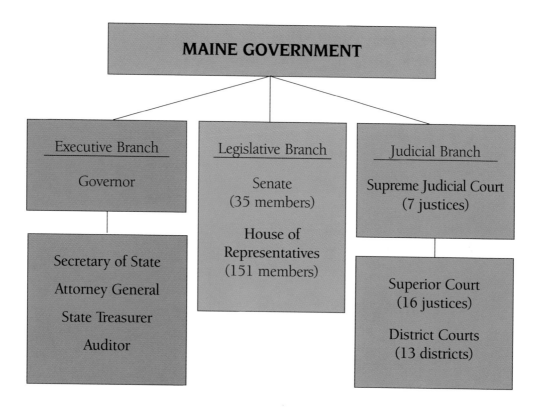

MAINE GOVERNMENT

Executive Branch

Governor

Secretary of State

Attorney General

State Treasurer

Auditor

Legislative Branch

Senate
(35 members)

House of
Representatives
(151 members)

Judicial Branch

Supreme Judicial Court
(7 justices)

Superior Court
(16 justices)

District Courts
(13 districts)

the state should spend its money. Maine's legislature is made up of two houses: a senate with 35 members and a house of representatives with 151 members. Each member of the legislature is elected by the public for two-year terms.

The legislature's most important task is to create bills—proposals for new laws. After a bill is approved in both the house and the senate, it lands on the governor's desk. If the governor signs the bill, it becomes law. If the governor vetoes it, the bill dies, unless two-thirds of the members of both houses vote to override the veto.

Judicial. The judicial branch hears legal cases and interprets state law. Maine's judicial system has three levels. At the lowest level are thirteen district courts, where many types of criminal and civil cases are heard. At the second level is the sixteen-member superior court, where a justice and jury hear serious criminal cases and important civil cases. A person who is dissatisfied with a decision made by a lower court may appeal to the superior court to get the ruling overturned. The supreme judicial court is at the highest level of all. It consists of a chief justice and six associate justices, whose main job is to hear cases appealed from lower courts. The governor appoints all judges on these courts to seven-year terms.

POLITICS IN ACTION

When it comes to politics, Mainers take pride in doing things their own way—even if it means bucking the nation's traditional two-party system. These days, the Pine Tree State actually has more Independent voters than Democrats or Republicans. Independents often provide the "swing vote" that decides whether a Democratic or Republican candidate wins. But politicians can also run on an Independent ticket. In 1974 and 1994 Maine elected Independent governors: James B. Longley and Angus S. King.

One recent Maine politician—a Democrat, in this case—made his greatest contribution after retiring from politics. After a distinguished career in the U.S. Senate, Waterville native George J. Mitchell was chosen to help find a solution to the long-running conflict between Protestant and Catholic factions in Northern Ireland. With his help, in 1998 the two sides signed a groundbreaking agreement that may bring lasting peace to this war-torn land.

Former senator George Mitchell, photographed with his wife and son, helped Northern Ireland negotiate a groundbreaking peace agreement in 1998.

FINDING A BALANCE

One big question dividing the state today is the same one that has challenged it for decades: How can Maine's natural resources be used in a way that brings the most benefit to everyone? Striking the right balance between providing jobs and preserving resources isn't easy. The problem often pits environmentalists against people in traditional Maine industries like fishing and logging—and the debates can get pretty heated.

In the mid-1990s, for example, environmental groups raised a storm of controversy by circulating a petition for a statewide ban on clear-cutting. More than 55,000 citizens signed it—enough to get the proposal on the ballot. "This really is a last-ditch effort to put brakes on the destruction of the north woods," said Jonathan Carter, a leading activist behind the measure. But most people in the lumber and wood products industries were against it, predicting business would suffer and thousands of workers would lose their

Logging is a leading industry in the Pine Tree State. It can be a big political issue, too. In the mid-1990s, Maine voters debated the pros and cons of clear-cutting, a controversial method of harvesting trees.

GROSS STATE PRODUCT: $31.4 BILLION

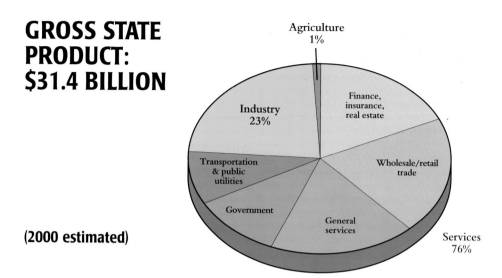

Agriculture 1%

Finance, insurance, real estate

Industry 23%

Transportation & public utilities

Wholesale/retail trade

Government

General services

Services 76%

(2000 estimated)

jobs. Calling the proposal a "gun to the head of the Maine economy," Governor Angus King got together with industry leaders and tried to persuade Mainers to vote it down.

At the polls, a majority of Mainers voted "no" on the clear-cutting ban. They also rejected a compromise measure, which would have reduced clear-cutting without stopping it altogether. Today, many people argue that clear-cutting is regulated enough already—around 5 to 10 percent of Maine's tree harvest is clear-cut these days. But that hasn't put an end to the controversy. In a state where thousands of people make a living from the woods—and where thousands more love to hike and camp there—taking care of the forests is bound to stay a big public issue for years to come.

MAINE AT WORK

The Pine Tree State has been through some hard times lately. Its economy surged in the 1980s, as an increase in U.S. military spending boosted employment at two of its biggest operations, the Bath and Kittery shipyards. But that boom was short-lived. In the early 1990s, the U.S. government signed fewer shipbuilding contracts and closed Loring Air Force Base—northern Maine's largest employer.

Stiff competition among world paper manufacturers made matters even worse. More than 100 people lost their jobs when Kimberly-Clark reduced production at its paper plant in 1996. The next year the plant closed down, laying off another 264 workers. "There's an old proverb," said Bruce Marshall, who was let go after

A frigate undergoes repairs at Bath Iron Works near Portland. Maine ship-yards get much of their business from the U.S. military.

EARNING A LIVING

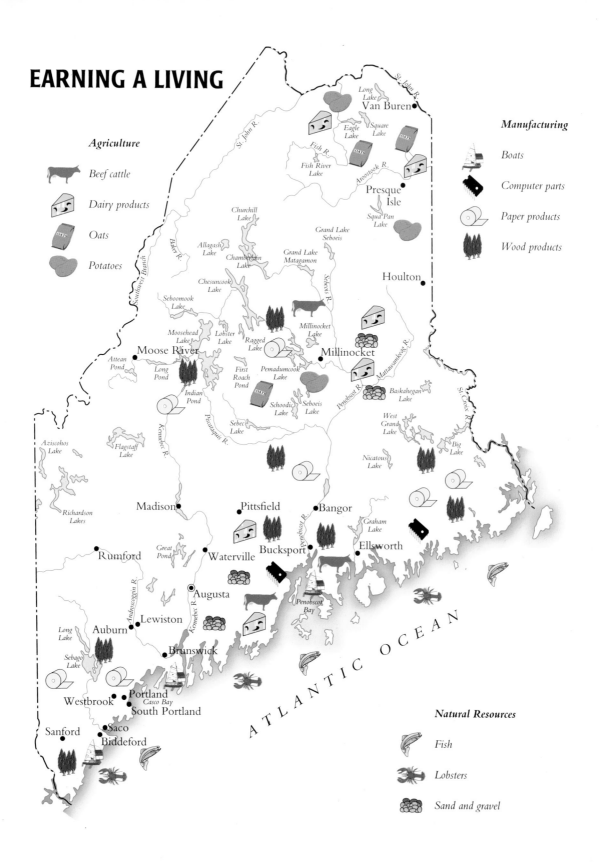

Agriculture

Beef cattle

Dairy products

Oats

Potatoes

Manufacturing

Boats

Computer parts

Paper products

Wood products

Natural Resources

Fish

Lobsters

Sand and gravel

Van Buren

Long Lake

St. John R.

Eagle Lake

Square Lake

Fish R.

Fish River Lake

Aroostook R.

Presque Isle

Squa Pan Lake

St. John R.

Churchill Lake

Grand Lake Seboeis

Houlton

Allagash Lake

Chamberlain Lake

Grand Lake Matagamon

Seboeis R.

Baker R.

Chesuncook Lake

Seboomook Lake

Moosehead Lake

Lobster Lake

Millinocket Lake

Millinocket

Mattawamkeag R.

Southwest Branch

Moose River

Ragged Lake

First Roach Pond

Pemadumcook Lake

Penobscot R.

Baskahegan Lake

Attean Pond

Long Pond

Indian Pond

Schoodic Lake

Seboeis Lake

West Grand Lake

St. Croix R.

Sebec Lake

Piscataquis R.

Kennebec R.

Nicatous Lake

Big Lake

Aziscohos Lake

Flagstaff Lake

Graham Lake

Madison

Pittsfield

Bangor

Ellsworth

Richardson Lakes

Great Pond

Waterville

Bucksport

Rumford

Androscoggin R.

Augusta

Penobscot Bay

Lewiston

Kennebec R.

Long Lake

Auburn

Brunswick

Sebago Lake

Westbrook

Portland

Casco Bay

South Portland

Sanford

Saco

Biddeford

ATLANTIC OCEAN

working for the company for twenty-eight years. "Anything man has made never lasts. And it's true. Cars don't last. Buildings don't last. Jobs don't last. But how many times do we have to change our lifestyle to stay in the state of Maine . . . to survive?"

Although prospects have brightened recently in the southern part of the state, much of northern Maine is still floundering. Unemployment rates in Washington County hovered around 10 percent in the year 2000, compared with about 3 percent in York County, south of Portland. Business can be so slow in the north, people often end up taking several jobs to get by, combining fishing with factory work or teaching with farming.

The lumbering and wood-processing industries are still the

Workers handle enormous rolls of paper at a mill in Rumford.

An Aroostook County farmer shows off stalks of freshly picked broccoli. Next to potatoes, broccoli is the County's biggest crop.

mainstay of the state's economy, employing about 30,000 Mainers. In addition to paper, trees cut from the Maine woods are used to produce plywood, shingles, furniture, Christmas trees and wreaths, and toothpicks.

Tourism is Maine's second-biggest industry. Coastal towns provide food, lodging, and transportation to summer vacationers, and western mountain towns host winter skiers and snowmobilers. Tourism can be big money, bringing $3 billion into the state each year.

Although it's not often thought of as an agricultural state, Maine farmers raise livestock and grow apples, broccoli, and almost

Winter campers huddle in a tent as shadows fall across a snow-covered field.
Outdoor recreation and tourism play a major role in the state's economy.

RECIPE: BLUEBERRY MUFFINS

Baked goods made from local blueberries are a popular treat in northern Maine, especially in the summertime. Have an adult help you make this recipe for a delicious Down East snack.

1 cup milk
1 egg
⅓ cup vegetable oil
2 cups all-purpose flour
2 teaspoons baking powder
½ cup sugar
1 cup blueberries (wild blueberries are the best!)

Preheat oven to 400 degrees. Grease a 12-cup muffin tin. Blend milk, egg, and oil in a large bowl. Add flour, baking powder, sugar, and blueberries and mix with just a few quick strokes. Don't overmix! That's the secret to great muffins.

Pour batter into muffin cups. Each cup should be about two-thirds full. Bake 20 minutes and serve fresh from the oven!

80,000 acres of potatoes, mostly in Aroostook County. Centered in coastal Washington County is Maine's sweetest crop—the small but tasty wild blueberry.

Two other historic Maine industries, fishing and lobstering, continue to support many of Maine's coastal towns, though fewer people make a living that way than they used to. The populations of cod, flounder, haddock, and other fish living along the New England coast have sunk so low over the past few years that strict limits have been placed on the amounts fishing boats can bring in. Maine's Atlantic cod catch, for example, dropped 80 percent between 1985 and 1998. To help get the numbers back up again, in 1999 the New England Fishery Management Council slashed the daily cod allowance off the Gulf of Maine from four hundred to two hundred pounds—putting a big dent in the coastal economy.

On the other hand, scientific studies aren't always successful in predicting the industry's ups and downs. Biologists have been warning lobstermen for years that their livelihood is about to disappear. But in 1998 Maine lobster traps took in 45.5 million pounds of lobster—like 1997, it was a bumper year. "The numbers don't surprise me," said one lobsterman. "I think it lends to the theory that there's too many damn lobsters out there."

These days, state leaders say attracting new businesses is the best way to keep the economy thriving, and that means Maine's economic makeup is destined to change. In some parts of the state, you can see the shift taking place already. Telemarketing, Maine's fastest-growing industry, now employs many of the people who once worked in manufacturing. And Internet companies are starting up in the Portland area and along the coast.

A deckhand sits by a pile of traps on a lobster boat making its rounds near Monhegan Island. More than 90 percent of the nation's lobsters are caught off the coast of Maine.

One thing the state has going for it is a pleasant environment, which makes it appealing to companies as well as "telecommuters"—people who do business from home using the Internet. Says one entrepreneur who recently moved from New York to Portland, "The fact is, this is a great place to live."

4 TOGETHER IN MAINE

A Texas man once told a Maine farmer, "Back home, I can get in my car and drive for three days and still not make it all the way around my ranch." "You don't say," replied the Mainer. "I had a car like that once." It's an old joke, but there's still a grain of truth to it: it's hard to impress a Mainer. Generally speaking, values like hard work, thrift, and honesty are more important to Down East folks than wealth and fancy possessions. Mainers are also known for speaking their minds without wasting a lot of words. Between their broad New England accents and conservative attitudes, long-time Mainers can sometimes seem a bit rough around the edges to people visiting the state for the first time. But after getting to know them better, most out-of-staters find that even the most crotchety Mainers can also be remarkably tolerant, fair-minded, and kind.

NATIVES AND FLATLANDERS

With its old New England heritage, Maine is anything but cosmopolitan. More than 98 percent of the state's residents are white. About 2 percent of the population are African-American, Hispanic, Asian-American, or Native American.

But if Maine isn't as diverse as some other states, that doesn't mean Mainers are all alike. Ask a few residents about their neighbors

Down East natives are known for their independent spirit. "Some people take the easy way and are born here," says one Maine newcomer. "The rest have to work hard to become Mainers."

and you'll begin to grasp the differences—even between people who look and act pretty much the same.

To start with, Mainers make a big distinction between year-round residents and "summer people." For more than a hundred years, people from farther south have been coming to Maine to spend the summers. Some families have been vacationing in the same spot for generations, often buying their own homes in Maine. Locals have gotten used to their summer neighbors, and relations between the two groups are generally polite and easygoing. Still, they usually keep to their separate worlds. Their differences can be a source of amusement, too. Year-round Mainers like to make gentle fun of the overindulged city folks, while for summer people, the crusty locals with their colorful accents are part of the season's charm.

Even being born in Maine and living there year-round doesn't necessarily make you a native in the minds of some old-time Mainers. In many communities, the same families have lived together for hundreds of years. When a new family moves in, it may take a generation or two before their neighbors think of them as locals. Instead, they'll likely be considered "flatlanders" or "people from away." Philadelphia native Ann Wilson's family moved to rural

A twelve-year-old lobster fisherman visits with a young neighbor.

THE BEAR AND THE SLICKER

Down East humor sometimes targets summer visitors—and sometimes plays on the blunders of Mainers themselves. Who has the last laugh in this traditional tale?

A city slicker was asked to go hunting with a group of Maine sportsmen. When the slicker said he couldn't bring himself to kill a harmless deer, they gave him a squirrel gun and told him to go off and find a bear. He struck off bravely into the woods, and before ten minutes were gone, he came upon what he was looking for. He dropped his gun and tore back to camp with the bear close on his heels. The slicker tripped on the cabin doorsill, and the bear tripped on him, rolling head over heels into the cabin. The slicker got up, dashed outside, slammed the door, and peering in the window, shouted, "There's your bear fellows. You skin him out, while I go back for more!"

Maine when she was three. "If you're a kid and you come from someplace else," remembers Wilson, "you either become an object of fascination, or you get called 'quee-ah'—which means weird."

ETHNIC MAINE

The oldest Maine families with European roots are of English, Scottish, and French heritage. These people came to the area when it was still a frontier, and many still make their living the way their ancestors did, fishing, lumbering, lobstering, or farming.

In the mid-nineteenth century, many people came to the state from poverty-stricken Ireland and Quebec, Canada, to find work in

Morris dancers practice an old English tradition at West Quoddy Head, near Lubec. Most Maine families have roots in the British Isles.

its mills and factories. These newcomers were not easily accepted at first. As Catholics they were looked down on by the state's strong Protestant majority. In time, though, they became as much a part of Maine as the industries they supported.

Maine is also home to many Scandinavian Americans. Finns came to work in the granite and slate quarries along the coast in the nineteenth century. And in 1870, fifty-one Swedes helped set up a model farming community in Aroostook County. Their descendants still live in the town they founded, New Sweden, as well as in nearby Stockholm. Each June during New Sweden's Midsommar Festival, residents celebrate the longest day of the year the Swedish way, with colorful costumes, music, dancing, and a smorgasbord— a banquet featuring traditional Scandinavian foods.

Americans of French heritage make up Maine's largest non-British ethnic group, accounting for nearly one-fourth of the state's population. Although most French-speaking Mainers in mill towns like Lewiston and Biddeford trace their roots to Quebec,

Scandinavian-American folk dancers show off brightly colored costumes at New Sweden's Midsommar Festival.

ETHNIC MAINE

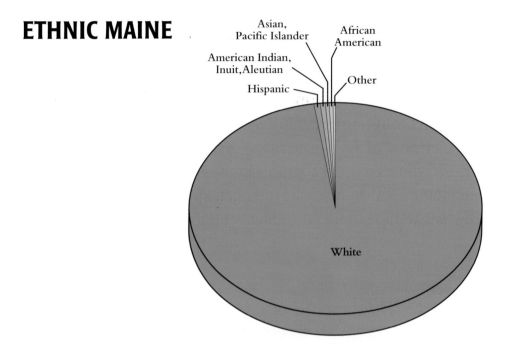

Asian, Pacific Islander

African American

American Indian, Inuit, Aleutian

Other

Hispanic

White

the oldest French communities go back to a different source. They were started by people from New Brunswick and Nova Scotia—colonies formed by France in the 1600s, when the land was still known as Acadia. Driven from their home by the British in 1755, many Acadians fled to the St. John River valley, where they established farms on the meager soil. Acadian culture has survived in towns like Van Buren, Frenchville, Fort Kent, and Madawaska, where you can still hear French spoken in the streets.

For all its variety, Maine is still a mostly "white" state, and that can make life a bit lonely for the African Americans who live there. Racial discrimination can be a problem, but many people of color say the worst issue they face is simple ignorance. Roy Partridge, an African-American Episcopal priest in Scarborough, has lived in

UNE FÊTE ACADIENNE

Each year at the end of June, the people of the St. John River valley dance to the music of their French forebears during the most popular cultural celebration in Maine, Madawaska's Acadian Festival. While fiddlers play lively Franco-American tunes, visitors can sample local specialties like *ployes* (buckwheat cakes), *poutine* (French fries with cheese and gravy), and *fougêre* (wild fiddlehead ferns). The four-day *fête* (festival) is also a reunion of sorts, since Madawaska honors a local family each year and invites long-lost relatives to return to their roots for a few days of Acadian-style *joie de vivre* (enjoyment of life).

Native American girls take part in an Aroostook County parade.

Maine for fourteen years. "People will ask me almost once a month: 'Are you from Maine?'" says Partridge. "What you get to experience is people saying, 'You're the first person of color I've ever known.'"

Maine's small population of Native Americans have faced many hardships, including high unemployment, alcoholism, and poverty. But these problems have eased since the Penobscot and the Passamaquoddy tribes went to court to get paid for the 12.5 million acres they lost to Massachusetts in 1794. In a landmark decision in 1980, the tribes were awarded $81.5 million. Since then, conditions have improved on the tribes' reservations. Older tribe members are

BASKETS, FANCY AND STRONG

Most Maine Native Americans live much as other Mainers do, and many of their grandparents' customs have been forgotten. But one Abnaki tradition is still alive and well: the ancient craft of basket making.

Centuries ago, Maine's first residents learned to pound ash logs until the wood could be peeled off in flexible strips and woven together to make sturdy baskets. From the islands they gathered sweetgrass, a supple, fragrant plant they dried and twisted into delicate patterns for decoration. When city folks first began vacationing in Maine, the Indians' baskets became popular as knickknacks in summer homes. Penobscot and Passamaquoddy basket makers soon started shaping their wares to meet customers' needs, making all kinds of fancy items from pillboxes to picture frames. Larger undecorated baskets became the specialty of the Micmac and Malecite, who sold them for use in fishing and potato harvesting.

Today, a small community of Abnaki basket makers carries on the tradition, drawing on their own creativity as well as skills learned from older members of the tribe. Prized by collectors, their work commands a much higher price than the Indians received at the end of the nineteenth century. But more important to most weavers is the chance to take part in a craft their families have passed down from generation to generation. As Passamaquoddy basket maker Sylvia Gabriel puts it, "We all learned from one another."

helping children learn the Passamaquoddy language. "We're working to keep our culture alive," says Joseph Nicholas. Each August the Passamaquoddy reservation at Pleasant Point, near Eastport, celebrates the tribe's heritage with Indian Days, a three-day festival featuring canoe races, crafts demonstrations, and traditional food and dancing.

NEW MAINERS

More recently, immigrants from far-off lands like Vietnam, Cambodia, Afghanistan, Somalia, Ethiopia, and the Sudan have begun to settle in Maine. Most of these newcomers came to the United

POPULATION GROWTH: 1800–2000

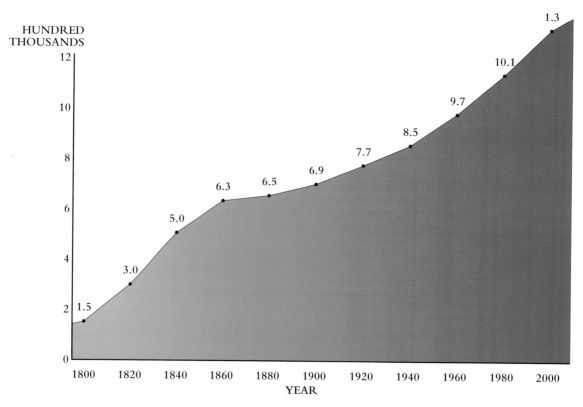

States to escape violent conflicts in their own countries and have been helped by a refugee resettlement program in Portland. Before the 1970s, Portlanders didn't have much contact with people from other parts of the world, so the growth of the city's international community has taken some adjustment on both sides. Portlander Ziba Nekooie, who came to Maine from Iran in 1978, says she sometimes gets impatient with longtime Mainers. "People have asked me, 'Are you a terrorist?' I've said, 'No, but my cousins are.' Once they hear you're from Iran, they want to start with the politics and I say, 'Please, I work all week, I just want to relax a couple hours. I don't represent a whole country.'"

At the same time, a lot of Mainers appreciate the way immigration has changed the face of Portland. "I like standing on Congress Street and seeing all the different kinds of people walking by," says twenty-seven-year-old Sarah Bernhard. "People in African garb, Rastafarians, people speaking different languages. It's really great."

ISLAND LIFE

All over the Pine Tree State, you'll find people who pride themselves on living in a remote, peaceful place far from the bothers of the city. But if you really want to know what solitude is all about, ask one of the 4,700 people who live year-round on the state's offshore islands. Even the toughest Down Easters agree island people are a breed apart—they pretty much have to be, considering the meager job prospects, severe winters, and physical isolation the islands guarantee. The history of these island communities stretches back hundreds of years, but the decline in fishing and shipping has taken its toll on their population in recent decades. Once there were three hundred Maine islands with full-time residents—now there are just fifteen.

The people who live on these last island outposts are known for their fierce independence. But they are also good at pulling together and helping each other get through the year. Some say that strong

Fog envelops a harbor on Swan's Island. To enjoy island life, says a teacher who works on nearby Long Island, "You must be independent and respect the way other people live."

feeling of community more than makes up for the loneliness of living offshore. New Jersey native Jackie Bell moved to Great Diamond Island in 1993. She and her husband experienced the island's close-knit community their very first week, when their electricity went out and five neighbors called to make sure they were OK. "Nobody in New Jersey would have called," she maintains. "We are deliriously happy here."

While a few island communities, like Matinicus Island, still subsist on fishing and lobstering, most depend at least partly on business from summer residents. The population of Great Chebeague Island, for example, swells from 325 to about 2,000 in midsummer. The yearly influx not only brings jobs, it also makes things more lively three months out of the year. "I love the winters here," says Alnah Robinson, a deckhand on the *Islander*, a ferry that serves Great Chebeague. "But come springtime, you're looking forward to seeing people again."

5 REMARKABLE MAINERS

A lot of talented people have roots in Maine. And no matter how far their achievements take them, that Down East spirit tends to stick with them. From best-selling novelists to big-time sports stars, many of Maine's most famous heroes still live in the state today.

LITERATURE

"I never wrote anything until I moved from Chicago to down-east coastal Maine," poet William Carpenter once said. Maine has a way of sparking the imagination. Some writers have found inspiration in its jagged shore, others in the solitude of the Great North Woods, still others in the peculiarities of small-town life in a state where the old New England ways linger.

One of the nineteenth century's most popular poets, Henry Wadsworth Longfellow, was born in Portland in 1807 and educated at Bowdoin College. Longfellow captivated readers with his sweeping poems about America. Works like *The Song of Hiawatha* and *The Courtship of Miles Standish* were translated into dozens of languages, and throughout his later life, he basked in international fame.

A generation later, author Sarah Orne Jewett won acclaim for her gentle portraits of the people and culture of rural Maine. The daughter of a country doctor, Jewett grew up in the 1850s in South

Henry Wadsworth Longfellow
was nineteenth-century
America's best-known poet.
He grew up in Portand,
"the beautiful town /
That is seated by
the sea."

Sarah Orne Jewett captured the
spirit of coastal Maine in her novel
The Country of Pointed Firs.

Best-selling horror writer Stephen King grew up in rural Maine and currently lives in Bangor.

Berwick, where she became a keen observer of local attitudes and manners. She longed to enter her father's profession, but she knew that as a woman, her chances of succeeding were slim. Instead she turned to writing, publishing her first story at age nineteen. Jewett's best-known work, *The Country of the Pointed Firs*, describes the strong, independent, and wistful inhabitants of Dunnet Landing, a fictional Maine village overlooking the sea.

Of today's Maine writers, no one thrills more readers than horror novelist Stephen King. A native of Portland, King started writing fiction at an early age. By the time he was fourteen, he had written his first book—a novelization of the 1961 movie *The Pit and the Pendulum*. Pleased with his work, he printed out copies on his brother's mimeograph machine. "In three days, I sold something like seventy of these things," he later wrote. "That was my first experience with bestsellerdom."

As a teenager, King spent hours alone in his room reading horror and science fiction paperbacks. He also wrote his own adventure stories, making friends and classmates into the heroes of his tales. After enrolling at the University of Maine at Orono, he wrote a weekly column for the school newspaper and began producing spine-tingling stories for magazines.

King was determined to become a professional author, and he never stopped writing, even when success seemed like a far-off dream. He and his family were living on almost nothing when he wrote *Carrie*, the story of a high school outcast with frightening supernatural powers. Published in 1974 and made into a block-buster movie in 1976, the book catapulted King to fame. Over the next twenty-five years, more than fifteen of his novels were turned into Hollywood films. King has lived in Bangor since 1980, and many of his books and movies, such as *Pet Sematary*, *Salem's Lot*, and *Needful Things*, are set in Maine.

REMAKING THE WORLD

Social reformer Dorothea Dix was born in Hampden in 1802, when Maine was still part of Massachusetts. As a young girl, she was sent to Boston to live with her grandmother, and at fourteen she started teaching at a girls' school in Worcester, Massachusetts. She later opened her own school in Boston, where she taught until a severe illness forced her to resign.

A MAINE POET

Poet Edna St. Vincent Millay was born in Rockland in 1892 and spent her childhood in Camden. When she was just nineteen, a summer visitor from New York "discovered" her. Millay left Maine to attend Vassar College and later moved to New York City's Greenwich Village, where she became one of the best-loved poets of her generation. This poem appeared in her 1921 book, *Second April*.

INLAND

People that build their houses inland,
People that buy a plot of ground
Shaped like a house, and build a house there,
Far from the sea-board, far from the sound

Of water sucking the hollow ledges,
Tons of water striking the shore,—
What do they long for, as I long for
One salt smell of the sea once more?

People the waves have not awakened,
Spanking the boats at the harbour's head,
What do they long for, as I long for,—
Starting up in my inland bed,

Beating the narrow walls, and finding
Neither a window nor a door,
Screaming to God for a death by drowning,—
One salt taste of the sea once more

After recovering her health in England, Dix returned to Boston to find that she had inherited a small fortune. Now comfortably well off, but still eager to make a contribution to the world, in 1841

In the mid-nineteenth century, social reformer Dorothea Dix led a tireless campaign to improve treatment of the mentally ill.

she began teaching a Sunday school class at the East Cambridge House of Correction. When Dix entered the prison, she was shocked by what she saw. Among the convicts were people who were clearly mentally ill. They were treated with unbelievable cruelty—left in dark, unheated cells without plumbing, and sometimes chained to the walls and beaten. Horrified, Dix began touring prisons and insane asylums all over the state. Finding the same brutal conditions again and again, in 1843 she wrote a detailed report and presented it to the Massachusetts legislature. Over the next few years, Dix's hard work and strong convictions helped persuade the state to reform its hospital and prison system.

Dix devoted the rest of her life to improving conditions for the mentally ill. Because she believed that all people should be treated humanely, she also fought for the rights of ordinary prisoners. Yet people who met her sometimes described her as cold. "I have no particular love for my species," she once claimed, "but own to an exhaustless fund of compassion."

PAINTING THE WAVES

Before Maine became a popular vacation spot, some of America's most talented artists discovered its wild beauty. Among the first to do so was Winslow Homer, a Boston native who began his career as an illustrator. In the 1860s, Homer won acclaim for his pictures documenting the Civil War, published in the magazine *Harper's Weekly*. But his fame spread even farther after he began painting his most compelling subject: the violence and mystery of the sea.

Homer bought property on Prout's Neck, just south of Portland, in 1883. Perched on the rocks there, he studied the waves, spellbound by their awesome power. He watched fishermen at work and noticed how the water reflected light as the weather changed and at different times of day. At Prout's Neck over the next three decades, Homer produced some of the most masterful works of his career. He captured the drama of nature in watercolors like *The Northeaster* and *Blown Away*, and the struggle for human survival in oil paintings such as *The Life Line*, which shows a woman being rescued from a wrecked ship during a storm at sea. "Homer painted the sea for the first time in history as it really looked," wrote fellow

Winslow Homer learned to paint the ocean by studying the light as it struck the waves at different times of day. "The Sun will not rise, or set, without my notice, and thanks," he wrote from his studio in Prout's Neck.

artist N. C. Wyeth after Homer's death in 1910. He is remembered today as one of America's finest artists.

RUNNING FOR THE GOLD

When Joan Benoit was a little girl, she dreamed of becoming a world-class skier. Bold, energetic, and fiercely dedicated, she might have become a star of the slopes if she hadn't broken her leg on a ski run at the age of sixteen. The accident shook her up so much she gave up her dream—and became a world-class runner instead.

Marathon runner Joan Benoit crosses the finish line at the 1984 Olympics in Los Angeles.

Joan Benoit was born in 1957 in Cape Elizabeth. She entered her first running competition when she was eight years old. While watching an older runner win the 880-yard dash, she noticed he kept his head and upper body still and his elbows close to his sides. Joan copied the style, ran five races—and came home with five blue ribbons!

Benoit began running cross-country races in high school, then trained even harder while studying at Bowdoin College and North

Carolina State University. On April 16, 1979, she entered the Boston Marathon—and won, beating the predicted champion, Patti Lyons, on the hilly, twenty-six-mile course, which is famed as one of track-and-field's most grueling events.

Exhilarated, Benoit set her sights on the 1984 Olympics in Los Angeles, where a women's marathon was to be held for the first time in the history of the games. During her training, she continued to perform well, winning the Boston Marathon again in 1983 with a world record time. One year later, she faced knee surgery just seventeen days before the Olympic trials. But by running cautiously, Benoit made the team, and in June she joined hundreds of the world's top women runners at Santa Monica College, where the Olympic marathon began.

Benoit started out running with the pack but soon broke away, keeping her lead right up to the twenty-sixth mile. As she stepped onto the ramp leading to the Los Angeles Coliseum and the finish line, she remembers thinking, "Once you leave this tunnel your life will be changed forever." Joan Benoit struck Olympic gold with a time of 2:24:52, a minute and a half ahead of the second-place runner.

"I look at victory as a milestone on a very long highway," Benoit once said. Now married and a mother of two in Freeport, she continues to run for the thrill and the challenge.

A MAINE OUTFITTER

Hunting, fishing, and trapping were a way of life in nineteenth-century Greenwood, the hometown of Leon Leonwood Bean. Born in 1872, L. L., as he was known to friends and family, spent much of his childhood tracking game in the Maine woods. He also showed a talent for business, selling his first buck to a pair of empty-handed hunters in his early teens. Bean's parents died when he was young, and he earned his way through school by selling soap. He eventually married a woman from Freeport, where he started a clothing store with his brother in 1905.

Bean loved the outdoors, but one thing exasperated him about it—while out tramping in the woods, his feet always got wet. Life in the woods would be so much better, he reasoned, if only he could get his hands on a pair of light, durable, water-resistant shoes. So he took a pair of rubber shoe bottoms from his store and

L. L. Bean turned his love of the outdoors into a booming business.

had a shoemaker stitch on a leather top. Pleased with his new product, he had more made up and sold a hundred pairs before realizing the rubber was too flimsy—all but ten of them were returned.

That first mishap didn't stop Bean. Instead, he paid a Boston manufacturer to turn out a better model. To get the word out about the new boots, he sold them by mail order. The "Bean boot" was the featured item in the first L. L. Bean catalog in 1912. As the sporting life became more popular, other hunting, fishing, and camping products were sold through the catalog as well. Pretty soon, L. L. Bean became the first name New Englanders thought of when they got ready to rough it. Customers would drop by Bean's store, located just above the Freeport post office with a mail chute leading directly down for fast delivery. So many hunters and fishers needed gear at odd hours of the morning that in 1951 Bean decided to keep the store open twenty-four hours.

From the start, Bean loved to hang out in the store and chat with customers, and his folksy style and backwoods know-how soon made him one of Maine's best-loved personalities. But it wasn't until after his death in 1967 that the business really soared. In the 1970s, the casual look featured in Bean's catalogues suddenly became a nationwide fad. By 1976 orders were coming in so fast the company got its own zip code. L. L. Bean has expanded twice since then, but some things haven't changed. Today's megastore still features many of the same hunting and fishing products Bean sold half a century ago. Look carefully between the flannel shirts and warm woolen sweaters and you can almost catch a glimpse of the lakes, woods, and rivers that make up the heart of Maine.

6 OUT AND ABOUT IN MAINE

People who visit Maine in the summertime often end up going back to the same spot year after year, whether it's a lakeside camp or a fishing village on a quiet cove. But plenty of surprises await those who are willing to explore the state a bit more. An ideal place to start is in Maine's biggest city, Portland.

CITY BY THE SEA

Downtown Portland lies on a crooked peninsula jutting out into Casco Bay, an area the Abnaki called Machigonne, meaning "Great Knee." Portland's motto, *Resurgam*, is Latin for "I shall rise." That's because the city has risen up from near destruction several times. In 1690, French and Indian soldiers attacked the English settlement at Fort Loyal, beside Portland Harbor, and wiped out about forty families. The next onslaught came in 1775, when British warships leveled three-quarters of what was even then Maine's largest town. After the American Revolution, Portland sprang back to become stronger and more prosperous than ever before. During Fourth of July festivities in 1866 the city met its third great disaster. While Portlanders reveled, a firecracker flew into a boatbuilder's yard and ignited a pile of wood shavings. Strong winds spread the blaze so quickly it soon demolished most of eastern Portland. The red brick and granite buildings that make up the Old Port district

A view of Portland from across the harbor

now were built in the 1870s and 1880s, after the fire.

Today, Portland is a thriving city of nearly 65,000, combining a host of urban attractions with the easygoing atmosphere of a small town. Its historic downtown boasts dozens of great restaurants, shops, parks, and museums. From the cafes of the city's Old Port neighborhood you can stroll out to the end of a dock and watch ships and fishing boats navigate the waters of Casco Bay. For an even more spectacular view, you might board a ferry to one of the bay's lovely islands or take a sunset whale-watching cruise.

The state's oldest and most renowned art museum, the Portland Museum of Art, is just a few blocks away. Its State of Maine collection features paintings by Winslow Homer, Rockwell Kent, Maurice Prendergast, and Andrew Wyeth, all of whom created some of their best-known works while summering in Maine.

Portland's historic houses show how the wealthiest Mainers lived

The Old Port district's red brick buildings preserve the flavor of days gone by.

PLACES TO SEE

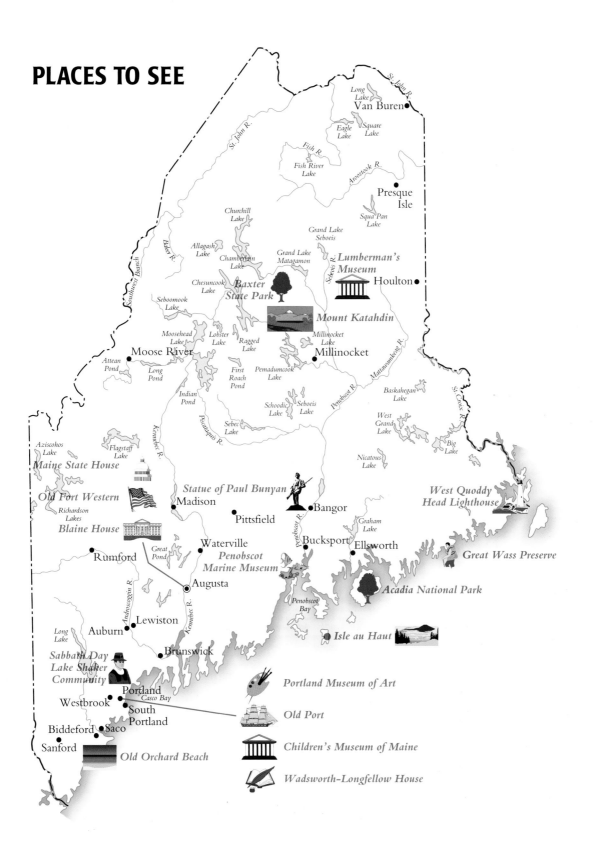

St. John R.

Long Lake

Van Buren

Eagle Lake
Square Lake

Fish R.

Fish River Lake

Aroostook R.

Presque Isle

Churchill Lake

Squa Pan Lake

Grand Lake Seboeis

Allagash Lake

Chamberlain Lake

Grand Lake Matagamon

Sebeois R.

Lumberman's Museum

Houlton

St. John R.

Baker R.

Chesuncook Lake

Baxter State Park

Mount Katahdin

Seboomook Lake

Southwest Branch

Moosehead Lake

Lobster Lake

Ragged Lake

Millinocket Lake

Millinocket

Mattawamkeag R.

Moose River

Attean Pond

Long Pond

First Roach Pond

Pemadumcook Lake

Baskahegan Lake

St. Croix R.

Indian Pond

Piscataquis R.

Schoodic Lake

Seboeis Lake

Penobscot R.

West Grand Lake

Big Lake

Aziscohos Lake

Flagstaff Lake

Sebec Lake

Nicatous Lake

Maine State House

Kennebec R.

Statue of Paul Bunyan

West Quoddy Head Lighthouse

Old Fort Western

Richardson Lakes

Blaine House

Madison

Pittsfield

Bangor

Graham Lake

Penobscot R.

Buckbsport

Ellsworth

Great Wass Preserve

Rumford

Great Pond

Waterville

Penobscot Marine Museum

Andascoggin R.

Augusta

Penobscot Bay

Acadia National Park

Long Lake

Auburn

Lewiston

Kennebec R.

Brunswick

Isle au Haut

Sabbath Day Lake Shaker Community

Portland

Casco Bay

Westbrook

South Portland

Biddeford

Saco

Sanford

Old Orchard Beach

Portland Museum of Art

Old Port

Children's Museum of Maine

Wadsworth-Longfellow House

in days gone by. The Wadsworth-Longfellow House, built by the grandfather of Henry Wadsworth Longfellow in 1785, was the city's first brick house. A tour takes you through rooms furnished in the style of the early nineteenth century, when the poet was a young boy. More lavish is the Victoria Mansion, an 1850s summer residence richly adorned with stained glass, velvet, marble, and mahogany.

One thing people love about Portland is that even though it has the feel of a city, the country is always right close by. Tucked amid the rolling hills of Cumberland County just to the north is a perfect example of old-fashioned farming life, the Sabbathday Lake Shaker Community. The Shakers are members of a religious order formed in the 1700s. Sabbathday Lake, founded in 1794, is now the only active Shaker community in the world. Though they number fewer than ten, its members still live according to the principles of simplicity, kindness, communal living, and equality that marked the Shakers' beginnings. A tour of Sabbathday Lake offers visitors a glimpse of life there in earlier times, when some of our most familiar household items, like the flat broom and the clothespin, were invented by Shaker craftsmen.

THE CAPITAL AND THE QUEEN CITY

Straddling the Kennebec River in the upland region is Maine's capital, Augusta. Government leaders meet under the copper dome of the Maine State House, whose original structure was built of local granite in 1832. Remodeled in the early twentieth century, it has some unusual features for a state capitol—including a stuffed

The mythical lumber-jack Paul Bunyan welcomes visitors to Bangor.

moose and a bronze plaque left by Governor Percival P. Baxter in memory of Garry, his faithful red setter. Another Augusta landmark, Old Fort Western, was built in 1754 as part of the British expansion into the Kennebec Valley. A summer visit to the fort today may include demonstrations of frontier arts practiced at the fort during colonial times.

Not far from the center of downtown Bangor stands a thirty-one-foot statue of the legendary giant lumberjack Paul Bunyan. It was lumber, after all, that earned Bangor the nickname Queen City in the nineteenth century, and locals claim the world's biggest logger was a real-live Mainer, born in Bangor on February 12, 1834. Elegant mansions built by lumber barons still grace the town's streets. One of the finest, protected by a wrought-iron gate bedecked with bats and cobwebs, belongs to best-selling horror author Stephen King.

DOWN EAST

A stunning section of the Maine coast can be found just south of Bangor on the Blue Hill Peninsula, overlooking Penobscot Bay. For a taste of old-fashioned island life, take the mailboat from the old granite-quarrying town of Stonington to scenic Isle au Haut. Half of this island belongs to Acadia National Park; the rest is shared by locals and summer people. On the park side, hiking trails will take you through the woods and along the shore, from one beautiful cove to another. Sit on a rock overlooking the ocean, listen to the waves toss, and watch the lobster buoys bob in the glittering water.

The main part of Acadia lies farther northwest on Mount Desert Island. Covering more than 40,000 acres of woods, lakes, camp-grounds, hiking trails, and rocky summits with dizzying views, this rugged playground attracts tourists all summer long. A great way to avoid big crowds is to walk or bike the carriage roads—a network of winding gravel paths that crisscross the park's eastern side. Some paths lead to the top of Cadillac Mountain. Others take hikers up more secluded peaks like Beech Mountain or toward dramatic

Hikers admire the view from the Great Head Trail in Acadia National Park.

sights like Somes Sound, a narrow cleft that nearly cuts the island in two.

On the northeast side of Mount Desert lies the old resort town of Bar Harbor. Before the Civil War, this was a sleepy fishing village called Eden—these days it's a mass of restaurants and motels. Most of the extravagant "cottages" that adorned Bar Harbor at the turn of the century were destroyed by a devastating fire in 1947. But here

A COUNTRY FAIR

One of the state's oldest agricultural fairs takes place each Labor Day weekend in the town of Blue Hill. It's a place where farm kids show off their best sheep, goats, cattle, and poultry, and oxen compete to see who can pull the heaviest load. With harness racing, a midway, a pig scramble, and a wild blueberry pie eating contest, the Blue Hill Fair sticks to down-home fun—it's one Maine tradition that's changed very little over the years. In 1938, New York writer E. B. White bought a farmhouse on Allen Cove, near Blue Hill. He quickly took to country life, and livestock shows at the Blue Hill Fair helped inspire his classic children's novel *Charlotte's Web*.

A tour boat docks near a seaside restaurant in Bar Harbor, Maine.

and there, you can still see traces of the estates where wealthy families like the Du Ponts and the Vanderbilts entertained.

Few tourists travel beyond Acadia to Washington County, Maine's loneliest stretch of shore. This unspoiled landscape of blueberry barrens, seaside villages, and rocky coastline spreads north and east to Cobscook Bay and the Canadian border. Near the sardine-fishing town of Lubec, red-and-white-striped West Quoddy Head Light stands guard over the easternmost place in the United States, an eighty-foot-high cliff perfect for spotting whales. A bit farther north, waters from the St. Croix River wrestle with the area's drastic tides to create "Old Sow," a treacherous whirlpool you can sometimes see from the ferry between Eastport and Deer Island, New Brunswick.

THE COUNTY

Aroostook County, the largest in the state, takes its name from a Micmac word meaning "bright" or "shining." Mainers often just

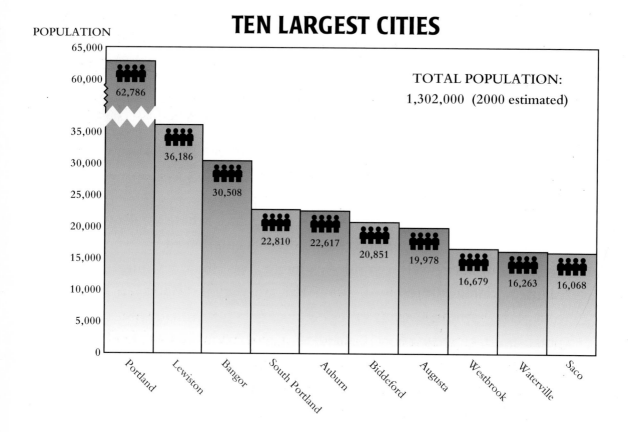

TEN LARGEST CITIES

POPULATION

TOTAL POPULATION: 1,302,000 (2000 estimated)

Portland 62,786
Lewiston 36,186
Bangor 30,508
South Portland 22,810
Auburn 22,617
Biddeford 20,851
Augusta 19,978
Westbrook 16,679
Waterville 16,263
Saco 16,068

Perched near the eastern tip of the United States, Lubec was once a major center for sardines. Today, aquaculture—raising fish and shellfish—is its fastest growing industry.

call it the County. Entering its wide-open spaces from the northeast coast means passing through the land where 90 percent of Maine's potatoes are grown. At Fort Fairfield's Potato Blossom Festival, held each July, locals celebrate the crop with a parade, mashed-potato wrestling, and a public potato supper, all surrounded by a sea of white, pink, and lavender blooms.

Mashed potato wrestling champs at the Maine Potato Blossom Festival

Starting in the town of Van Buren, a string of tidy farming communities with grand Catholic churches marks Acadian country, the French-speaking region of the St. John River valley. With its signs in both French and English and local French customs, this part of the state has a different flavor from any other—residents call it *chez nous* ("our place"). On the bank of the St. John near Madawaska, a fourteen-foot marble cross marks the spot where the Acadian founders first landed after their journey from Nova Scotia.

FORESTS, LAKES, AND STREAMS

It can take quite a while to get from the top of the state to Baxter State Park, in the center—miles and miles of forest cover the land in between. A good stopping place, the Lumberman's Museum in Patten, shows what life used to be like for the men who harvested this vast timberland. The museum's nine buildings contain everything from life-size logging camps to giant saws to sleds for

A guide demonstrates table manners at the Lumberman's Museum in Patten. Loggers were required to eat in silence, finish quickly, and get out of the cook's way so he could prepare the next meal.

BEANHOLE BEANS

Tourists may rave about lobster and blueberry pie, but to Mainers, nothing says summer more than a Saturday night supper of beanhole beans. The cooking method for this delicious dish goes back to colonial times, when the Penobscot Indians prepared their food in much the same way.

On Friday afternoon, the cook digs a hole in the ground a couple of feet deep, lights a wood fire in the bottom, and gives the beans a quick boil in an iron pot while the blaze dies down to glowing embers. After the beans are flavored with salt pork, mustard, and molasses, the pot goes into the hole with a lid on top, gets covered with dirt, and sits there overnight and all the next day. At about 5 P.M. on Saturday, the beans, baked to perfection, are carefully dug up and served.

Most small towns in Maine host public suppers featuring beans cooked in a hole in the ground. For a few dollars, you can try them yourself—and see if you agree that nothing compares to the taste of beanhole beans.

dragging logs through deep winter snows. Photographs of grizzled lumbering crews tell of the high risk and hard labor behind the boom years of the nineteenth century, when Bangor sent more than eight billion board feet of timber around the world.

Life can still be pretty rugged to the west of here, in the untamed wilderness of Baxter State Park. A narrow dirt road takes you from one end of the park to the other. No pets, radios, or cell phones are allowed, and visitors have to bring in their own drinking water. Rules are strict, but because they are, there's no better place to experience the Maine woods. If you arrange things ahead with a park ranger, you can hike up to a lake where you can borrow a canoe, paddle across, and then hike on to a waterfall before hiking and canoeing back again. Stay quiet and you might meet a moose along the way.

It takes a full day to hike Mount Katahdin, but those who do are rewarded with unbelievable views. Writer Henry David Thoreau never made it to the top, but from above the treeline, he marveled at the scene below: "I could see the country eastward, boundless forests, and lakes, and streams, gleaming in the sun. . . . Now and then some small bird of the sparrow family would flit away before me, unable to command its course, like a fragment of the gray rock blown off by the wind."

With forty-six mountain peaks and 175 miles of hiking trails, you could spend a whole lifetime exploring Baxter. But our tour ends here, at the Mountain of the People of Maine.

A moose comes up for air after grazing on underwater leaves. It isn't hard to find one of these gangly creatures in Baxter State Park, just listen for the sound of munching.

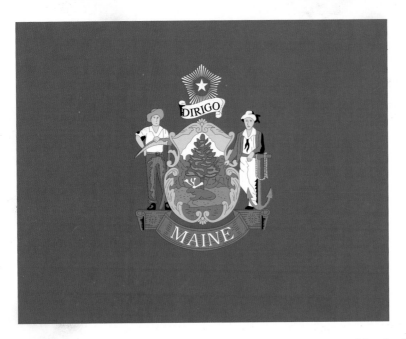

THE FLAG: The state flag depicts the state seal against a blue background. The flag was adopted in 1909.

THE SEAL: The state seal shows a farmer and a seaman, who represent agriculture, fishing, and shipping, three important industries in Maine. Between them is a shield depicting a pine tree and a moose, which symbolize the state's forests and wildlife. The state seal was adopted in 1820.

STATE SURVEY

Statehood: March 15, 1820

Origin of Name: Perhaps from the term *mainland*. Early explorers called the mainland the Main to distinguish it from offshore islands.

Nickname: Pine Tree State

Capital: Augusta

Motto: I direct

Bird: Chickadee

Flower: White pine cone and tassel

Tree: White pine

Fish: Landlocked salmon

Chickadee

White pine

STATE SONG

This rousing march was adopted as the official state song in 1937.

Words and Music by Roger Vinton Snow

Oh, Pine Tree State, Your woods, fields and hills, Your lakes, streams and rock - bound coast will ev - er fill our hearts with thrills. And tho' we seek far and wide, Our search will be in vain To find a fair - er spot on earth than Maine! Maine! Maine!

Insect: Honeybee

Gemstone: Tourmaline

Animal: Moose

GEOGRAPHY

Highest Point: 5,268 feet above sea level, at Mount Katahdin

Lowest Point: sea level along the coast

Area: 33,128 square miles

Greatest Distance, North to South: 303 miles

Greatest Distance, East to West: 202 miles

Bordering States: New Hampshire to the southwest

Hottest Recorded Temperature: 105°F at North Bridgton on July 10, 1911

Coldest Recorded Temperature: 48°F in Van Buren on January 19, 1925

Average Annual Precipitation: 41 inches

Major Rivers: Allagash, Androscoggin, Kennebec, Machias, Penobscot, Saco, St. Croix, St. John

Major Lakes: Chesuncook, Flagstaff, Millinocket, Moosehead, Pemadumcook, Rangeley, Sebago

Trees: balsam fir, basswood, beech, cedar, hemlock, maple, oak, pine, spruce, white birch, yellow birch

Wild Plants: anemone, aster, bittersweet, black-eyed Susan, buttercup, goldenrod, harebell, hepatica, jack-in-the-pulpit, lady's slipper, lavender, mayflower, wild lily

Animals: beaver, black bear, bobcat, harbor seal, lynx, marten, mink, moose, porcupine, raccoon, red fox, white-tailed deer

Harbor seal

Birds: bunting, duck, grackle, loon, osprey, owl, sparrow, spruce grouse, swallow, thrush, wren

Fish: alewife, bass, brook trout, cod, flounder, hake, mackerel, perch, pickerel, pollock, salmon, tuna

Endangered Animals: eastern puma, finback whale, humpback whale, leatherback sea turtle, right whale, roseate tern, shortnose strugeon

Endangered Plants: furbish lousewort

Roseate tern

TIMELINE

Maine History

c. 2500 B.C. Paleo-Indians known as the Red Paint people live in what is now Maine

c. A.D. 1000 Vikings from Norway visit Maine

1400s Abnaki, Passamaquoddy, Penobscot, Malecite, and Micmac Indians live in what will become Maine

1498 Explorer John Cabot reaches the Maine coast

1604 Frenchman Samuel de Champlain explores and names Mount Desert Island

1607 Englishmen in Maine build the *Virginia*, the first boat built by the English in what is now the United States

1620s The English begin settling Maine

1631 Maine's first sawmill is constructed

1677 Massachusetts gains control of Maine

1775 The American Revolution begins; the first naval battle of the war takes place off of Machias on the Maine coast

1785 The *Falmouth Gazette*, Maine's first newspaper, begins publication

1794 Bowdoin College, the first college in Maine, is established in Brunswick

1819 Mainers vote to separate from Massachusetts

1820 Maine becomes the 23rd state

1832 Augusta becomes the state capital

1833 Bath Iron Works opens

1836 Maine's first railroad is built

1842 The Webster-Ashburton Treaty ends a dispute over the border between Canada and Maine

1851 Maine becomes the first state to outlaw the sale of alcohol

1861–1865 About 72,000 Mainers serve in the Union army during the Civil War

1866 A fire destroys much of Portland

1923 Mainer Edna St. Vincent Millay wins the Pulitzer Prize in poetry

1924 WABI, Maine's first radio station, begins broadcasting in Bangor

1928 Acadia National Park is established

1941 The United States enters World War II

1948 Mainer Margaret Chase Smith becomes the first woman elected to the U.S. Senate

1969 Maine enacts a state income tax

1980 The Passamaquoddy and Penobscot Indians receive more than $80 million for land seized in the 18th and 19th centuries

1999 Edwards Dam is removed in an effort to restore fish populations in the Kennebec River

ECONOMY

Agricultural Products: apples, beef cattle, blueberries, chickens, eggs, hay, milk, oats, potatoes

Manufactured Products: boats, electrical components, food products, leather products, lumber, paper products

Natural Resources: clams, fish, forests, granite, limestone, lobsters, sand and gravel

Business and Trade: banking, insurance, real estate, telemarketing, tourism, wholesale and retail trade

Clams

CALENDAR OF CELEBRATIONS

New Year's Portland Thousands of Portlanders bundle up warmly and head out on New Year's Eve to enjoy music, dance, and comedy performances and a big fireworks display at midnight.

U.S. National Toboggan Championships Hundreds of teams from around the country race down a 400-foot chute at the toboggan championships in Camden each February.

Maine Maple Sunday All across the state on one March Sunday, sugarhouses making maple syrup invite visitors in to enjoy the tasty treat.

Old Port Festival Portland is filled with music each June when six stages are set up, each for a different type of music. Festivalgoers can listen to smooth jazz for a while and then take in some foot-stomping country. Besides all the music, you might want to check out the parade, which has lots of musicians and puppets, and try your hand at some games.

Annual Windjammer Days You can get a feel for what Maine looked like in centuries gone by when tall ships sail into Boothbay Harbor each June. Besides watching the graceful old boats, you can take in a concert, a dance, and fireworks and maybe even tour a navy boat.

La Kermesse Festival One of the nation's largest celebrations of Franco-American culture happens in Biddeford each June. A fireworks display starts the event off with a bang, and then there's a big parade. You might also want to try such traditional foods as crepes (thin pancakes), tourtiére (pork pie), and boudin (blood sausage).

Great State of Maine Air Show Each July, 200,000 people show up in Brunswick to watch some of the nation's best stunt flying teams. The show also includes displays of dozens of military aircraft. You can even sit in the cockpit of some of them.

Maine Lobster Festival Eat your fill of Maine's favorite food at what may be the world's largest lobster feed in Rockland each August. There's also a parade and a rollicking clam-shucking contest and race across lobster crates.

Maine Festival Musicians and dancers from around the nation and food from around the world will vie for your attention at this four-day extravaganza in Brunswick each August.

Blueberry Festival August is harvesttime for the wild blueberries that grow near Machias. At this festival, you'll end up with a full stomach and blue lips.

Blueberry pie-eating contest

Annual Great Falls Balloon Festival Dozens of huge hot air balloons set sail above Lewiston each August. If you want to get into the air yourself, balloon and helicopter rides are available.

Harvest Fest At this old-fashioned festival in York Village in October, you can enjoy an ox roast, hay rides, and lots of music.

Christmas Prelude Santa arrives in a lobster boat at this December event in Kennebunkport that kicks off the holiday season. Fairgoers can also eat their fill at a pancake breakfast, enjoy some caroling, and then tour the picturesque town.

STATE STARS

L. L. Bean (1872–1967), who founded one of the nation's leading outdoor gear retailers, was born in Greenwood. Early on, Bean became famous for the "Bean boot," a shoe he devised with a rubber bottom and leather top, which is both lightweight and keeps your feet dry. Over the years, so much of Bean's business came from catalog orders that his store eventually got its own zip code. Today, shoppers look to L. L. Bean for comfortable, casual clothing as well as outdoor gear.

Joan Benoit (1957–   ), a native of Cape Elizabeth, won the first women's Olympic marathon at the 1984 games in Los Angeles. Benoit's first major marathon victory came in 1979 when she captured the prestigious Boston marathon. She triumphed again in Boston in 1983 in world-record time. The year after winning Olympic gold, Benoit earned the James E. Sullivan Memorial Award for the nation's outstanding amateur athlete.

William Cranch Bond (1789–1859) was an early leader in American astronomy. Bond began his career as a watchmaker, but an eclipse of the sun in 1806 captured his imagination. In 1839 he established the Harvard College Observatory in Massachusetts, which became a center of astronomical research during his many years as director there. Bond is credited with discovering the dark ring of the planet Saturn and Hyperion, one of Saturn's moons. He also improved photography techniques for astronomy, taking the first photos of stars and better shots of the moon than ever before. Bond was born in Falmouth.

Robert Tristram Coffin (1892–1955), a poet from Brunswick, earned a 1936 Pulitzer Prize for his book *Strange Holiness*. In his poetry, he often described the sights and sounds and people of the Maine seacoast. Coffin also wrote a novel, *Lost Paradise*, which re-created his Maine boyhood.

William Cohen (1940–   ) has been a U.S. senator, representative, and secretary of defense. A native of Bangor, Cohen served on the Bangor City Council before Mainers sent him to Washington, D.C., in 1973. A strong supporter of the military, Cohen became the first Republican nominated to be secretary of defense by a Democrat when President Bill Clinton tapped him for the job in 1997. Cohen's interests extend beyond politics.

He has written poetry and several spy novels, including *The Double Man*.

William Cohen

Cyrus H. K. Curtis (1850–1933), a Portland native, founded the Curtis Publishing Company, which produced such magazines as the *Saturday Evening Post* and *Ladies' Home Journal*. Curtis began his publishing career at age 15, when he began putting out a four-page weekly called *Young America*. His first big success came in 1879, when he began publishing *Tribune and Farmer*. Four years later he started printing the paper's women's page separately as *Ladies' Home Journal*. It soon became one of the nation's most popular magazines. Curtis later bought such newspapers as the *Philadelphia Public Ledger* and the *Philadelphia Inquirer*.

Cyrus H. K. Curtis

Dorothea Dix (1802–1887) was a social reformer who worked to improve the treatment of prisoners and the mentally ill. Dix first became interested in these causes in 1841, when she began teaching Sunday school at a prison and was horrified by the conditions there. She discovered that many of the prisoners were mentally ill and that they were often chained and beaten. Dix began campaigning for changes in the treatment of the insane. Because of her, institutions for the insane were established in 20 states and Canada. Her work also resulted in major prison reforms in Europe. Dix was born in Hampden.

Marsden Hartley (1877–1943) was an artist from Lewiston who often painted Maine landscapes. In 1912 Hartley went to Europe. Influenced by the artists there, he became one of the first Americans to make abstract paintings rather than works that show specific objects or scenes. By 1920 he was again painting pictures of Maine, but in a different way. In his later works, the people and places were simplified, with strong outlines and bold colors. Among the most famous of these is his 1941 painting *Lobster Fishermen*.

Marsden Hartley

Winslow Homer (1836–1910) was among the greatest 19th-century American painters. Born in Boston, Homer spent some of his childhood in Maine. Early in his career he often painted pleasant scenes of children and farm life. But he is most famous for the intense seascapes and fishermen he painted after moving to Prout's Neck on the Maine coast in 1883. These paintings often have dramatic contrast between dark and light and show people struggling against the power of nature.

Sarah Orne Jewett (1849–1909) wrote colorful but honest stories about rural Mainers. Jewett was born in South Berwick, the scene of many of her stories. Her books include *The Country of the Pointed Firs* and *Deephaven*.

Stephen King (1947–   ), perhaps the world's most widely read horror novelist, is famed as a brilliant storyteller who can produce spellbinding novels year after year. King often writes about everyday situations that turn terrifying. In his first novel, *Carrie*, a high school girl uses her supernatural powers to get revenge on classmates. *Carrie*, *The Shining*, *Misery*, and many of King's other books have been turned into popular films. King was born in Portland.

Henry Wadsworth Longfellow (1807–1882) was one of the most popular poets of the 19th century. Using clear, simple language and musical rhythms, Longfellow wrote such classics as "Paul Revere's Ride" and *The Song of Hiawatha*. He was born in Portland and attended Bowdoin College.

Hiram Maxim (1840–1916), an inventor from Sangerville, designed the first practical automatic machine gun, as well as an automatic sprinkler and an electric current generator. Some of Maxim's early inventions involved electric lights. After losing a lawsuit over a patent to Thomas Edison, the man credited with inventing the electric lightbulb, Maxim moved to England. Later in his career, he experimented with building internal combustion engines for cars and planes.

Hiram Maxim

Edna St. Vincent Millay (1892–1950) won the 1923 Pulitzer Prize in poetry for *The Ballad of the Harp Weaver*. Millay was known for using traditional poetic forms to express strong emotions about love and death. In her later works, Millay showed more interest in history. For instance, the poems in her 1937 collection *Conversation at Midnight* deal with events that would lead to World War II. Millay was born in Rockland.

George Mitchell (1933–   ) is a politician from Waterville. After working as a lawyer and a judge, Mitchell was elected to the U.S. Senate in 1980. He retired in 1995, but did not stay out of the public eye for long. Instead, he was tapped to chair peace talks in Northern Ireland, where Protestant and Catholic factions had long been in conflict. With his patience and willingness to listen, he became trusted by all sides and was able to hammer out a treaty in 1998 that brought the hope of peace to the war-torn region.

George Mitchell

Edmund Muskie (1914–1996) was the first Democrat Mainers ever elected to the U.S. Senate. Muskie, a native of Rumford, served in the Maine house and as the state's governor before being elected to the U.S. Senate in 1959. In 1968, Muskie was chosen as the Democratic vice presidential candidate, but the Republicans won that year. Throughout his career Muskie was known for fighting pollution and promoting education.

Edmund Muskie

Louise Nevelson (1900–1988) was an artist renowned for her abstract wooden sculptures. Nevelson worked in many styles and materials before making her most famous works in wood in the 1950s. She is perhaps best-known for her so-called sculptural walls, boxes set on end containing objects such as wheels and chair slats. Nevelson was born in the Ukraine and moved with her family to Rockland in 1905.

Louise Nevelson

Margaret Chase Smith (1897–1995) was the first woman to be elected to both the U.S. House and the U.S. Senate. Smith, a Republican born in Skowhegan, entered the House in 1940 and was elected to the Senate in 1948. She became highly respected for speaking out against anything she viewed as extremist. For example, she was one of the first senators to oppose Senator Joseph McCarthy, who was waging a campaign against people he said were communists. In 1964 Smith made history again when she became the first woman to vie for a major party's presidential nomination.

Margaret Chase Smith

E. B. White (1899–1985) wrote the classic children's books *Charlotte's Web* and *Stuart Little*. He was also one of America's most influential essayists, writing simple, elegant, and amused pieces for such prestigious magazines as the *New Yorker* and *Harper's*. White, who was born in New York, moved to Allen Cove in 1938.

E. B. White

Kate Douglas Wiggin (1856–1923) wrote *Rebecca of Sunnybrook Farm*, a classic novel about a spirited girl from a poor family. The novel is set in a village very similar to Hollis, Maine, the town where Wiggin grew up. Besides writing, Wiggin also worked to improve the education of America's children. In 1878 she established the first kindergarten on the West Coast, and two years later she founded the California Kindergarten Teacher Training School.

Andrew Wyeth (1917–   ) is an artist who has often painted landscapes of Maine. Wyeth, the son of painter and illustrator N. C. Wyeth, was born in Pennsylvania but during his childhood spent his summers in Maine. As an adult, he lived in Cushing. Wyeth's realistic paintings, which are often bathed in browns and grays, are immensely popular. In 1970 he became the first living artist to have an exhibition at the White House. One of his most famous works, *Her Room*, hangs in the Farnsworth Museum in Rockland, Maine.

Andrew Wyeth

TOUR THE STATE

Old Gaol Museum (York) You can visit the jail cells where some of Maine's earliest criminals were kept. Built in 1719, it is the oldest English public building in Maine.

Old Orchard Beach (Old Orchard Beach) After relaxing on the fabulous sandy beach, you might want to head up to the amusement park and pier for some rides and games.

Seashore Trolley Museum (Kennebunkport) Hop on a historic trolley for a four-mile ride. Then take a look at some of the 250 other trolleys from around the world housed at this unusual museum.

Penobscot Marine Museum (Searsport) This fascinating museum includes several historic buildings, including a sea captain's house where you can learn all about the lives of seamen, both at work and at home. Also on display are navigational instruments, sailing charts, and ship models.

Portland Head Light (Portland) Some people say this is the most photographed lighthouse in the country. It's hard to say if that's true, but having been built in 1791, it's certainly one of the oldest.

Portland Museum of Art Lots of works by artists with Maine connections including Winslow Homer and Andrew Wyeth are exhibited at Maine's largest art museum.

Blaine House (Augusta) Today the governor lives in this beautiful 28-room mansion, but when it was built in the 1830s it was home to a sea captain.

Musical Wonder House (Wiscasset) This grand mansion built in 1852 is filled with antique music boxes, player pianos, Victrolas, and other musical machines.

Shore Village Museum (Rockland) You can see the nation's largest collection of lighthouse artifacts at this unusual museum.

Isle au Haut Rocky cliffs, dense forests, and pounding waves greet hikers on this small island.

Acadia National Park (Mount Desert Island) This is one of the nation's most popular national parks, and with its dramatic mountains, rocky coasts, and magnificent vistas, it's easy to see why. Folks come from all over to hike, bike, canoe, sea kayak, rock climb, or just enjoy the incredible scenery.

Great Wass Preserve (Beals) Hikers will pass through bogs, forests, and coasts in this magical and often misty spot.

Allagash Wilderness Waterway (Allagash) Remote and spectacular, this is considered the best canoe trip in Maine.

Patten Lumberman's Museum (Patten) You'll learn all about the lumberman's life at this site, which includes a rebuilt logging camp from the early 1800s, old machinery, and fantastic old photos of lumbermen.

Baxter State Park (Millinocket) Visitors flock to this park to climb Mount Katahdin, the highest peak in the state. But those who want to get away from the crowds will have no trouble finding peaceful places to hike and canoe and perhaps even spy a moose.

Norlands Living History Center (Livermore) Few places deserve the title "living history center" as much as this spot, where visitors are sent back into the 19th century. Those who spend the weekend help out on the farm, cook in the old-fashioned way, and even attend class in the tiny one-room schoolhouse.

Grinding coffee

FUN FACTS

Maine produces more toothpicks than any other state.

William Phips, who was born in 1650 near Woolwich, became the first

British knight born in America. He was knighted by King James II of England for finding treasure in the Bahamas.

Norway pines, which were once considered the best trees to use as the masts of ships, were not named for the country but for Norway, Maine. Lots of these magnificent trees grew near the town.

FIND OUT MORE

There's a lot more to learn more about Maine. You might start by checking your local library or bookstore for these titles.

GENERAL STATE BOOKS

Kent, Deborah. *Maine.* Chicago: Children's Press, 1999.

Thompson, Kathleen. *Maine.* Austin, TX: Raintree/Steck Vaughn, 1996.

BOOKS ABOUT PEOPLE AND PLACES IN MAINE

Dean, Julia. *A Year on Monhegan Island.* New York: Ticknor & Fields Book for Young Readers, 1995. A look at how the residents of a small Maine island work together throughout the year.

Fendler, Donn. *Lost on a Mountain in Maine.* Magnolia, MA: Peter Smith Pub., 1993. True story of a twelve-year-old boy lost for nine days on Mount Katahdin.

Goodman, Susan E. *Ultimate Field Trip 3: Wading into Marine Biology.* New York: Atheneum Books for Young Readers, 1999. A middle school class from Boston visits Cobscook Bay, Maine, to learn about the marine biology of the bay's tidal zone.

Kress, Stephen W., and Pete Salmansohn. *Project Puffin: How We Brought Puffins Back to Egg Rock.* Gardiner, ME: Tilbury House Publishers, 1997.

FICTION

White, E. B. *Charlotte's Web.* New York: HarperTrophy, 1999.

—. *Stuart Little.* New York: HarperTrophy, 1999.

Wiggin, Kate Douglas. *Rebecca of Sunnybrook Farm.* London: Puffin, 1985. An energetic ten-year-old girl goes to live with her aunt in a small Maine town.

WEBSITES

Maine Home Page: *http://www.state.me.us/*

Maine Office of Tourism: *http://www.visit-maine.com*

INDEX

Page numbers for illustrations are in boldface.